GAYS

To m—
Fu—

Mary E. tenoglu

Eggs In My Pocket

By

Mary Elizabeth Fenoglio

Published by

Synergy Solutions, Inc.
Florence, Texas

Printed in the U. S. A.

First Printing , 2008

ISBN
978-0-615-17082-4

Dedication

My Granma raised me, and every day of my life I hear her voice in my heart. She was an uneducated woman by the world's standards, and the smartest person I have ever known. Her approach to life, dedication to those really important things that have real practical and spiritual impact on those around her and the few demands she placed on others made an indelible impression on me. She always believed I could do anything I really wanted to do. This book is for her.

My Grandma

Contents

Acknowledgements

While they were not directly involved in the development of this book, I must acknowledge the opportunity given to me by Linda Scarborough and Clark Thurman, owners of the *Williamson County Sun*. Being hired as a stringer to write the Florence News column ultimately opened the door for *Eggs In My Pocket*.

The switch from the "news" column to the *Eggs* column as it is today has to be credited to Amy Burroughs, Editor of the *County Sun* from 2003 to 2007. She suggested a change in focus, which delighted me and caused a whole new population to begin reading the column. The *Eggs In My Pocket* heading sparked the interest of a very diverse and broad based population. Attracted perhaps by the column's name, readers indicate that they find the content interesting, sometimes controversial, often plain spoken and relative to their own lives. Many of them have memories of growing up on the farm, or of summers as children visiting grandparents on the farm. Through reading *Eggs In My Pocket*, they revisit a happy time in their lives.

Rebecca Robins, Editor of the *County Life* section of the paper, always encouraged the direction of the column and shared with me the many letters and comments the paper began to receive about the column and its content. The support and encouragement of both Amy and Rebecca was an invaluable part of the developing success of the column.

Then there are the constant inspirations that wind up as fodder for the writing; my family, both human and animal. From my pushface pack to my always energetic grandchildren, my flocks of birds to the gregarious goat herd, they surround me with their energy and antics, giving me daily inspiration. Papa and I are a fortunate couple who, partly by design and partly due to luck, have our children and grandchildren nearby. We all have our homes on the farm, separated by enough distance to allow for everyone's independence but close enough for the youngsters to walk from one place to the other if they choose to do so. The young Mothers worked, so the toddler grandsons, born just one day apart, were at home with Papa and Gigi. At about the time the boys started pre-school classes, 8-month old Sara came into our lives as the adopted daughter of our daughter. There was never a shortage of stories while they were at home and even now, when they are all in school, they still provide rich layers to our lives that often wind up in the column.

The farm and the animals we love have all provided endless enrichment to our daily lives, expressed in *Eggs*. We are close to the rhythm of the seasons swinging past, aware of the land and of life renewing itself endlessly, sunrise after sunset, steady and secure, bringing us hope even in the face of the relentless encroachment of urbanization into our way of life.

Last but not least, I must credit the person with whom I have shared over 50 years of married life for his support and encouragement through our lives together. His approach to life and work and his tolerance of my affinity for animals and totally diverse priorities have made my life most days much easier than it might have been otherwise. On those days – and they are many - that challenge my ability to cope, he has been a rock. This book would very likely have remained just one more "around-to-it" were it not for Papa. To him I give my thanks and my love.

And to the readers of the column, I say "Thank you!" and "Enjoy!"

Introduction

We transplanted our family from the suburbs to the rural life more than thirty years ago, young townies (a term fully explained on my website www.eggsinmypocket.com) full of naiveté, more enthusiasm than experience, and way more optimism than the actual facts of our new circumstances would warrant. As a family we learned some poignant lessons in the school of hard knocks, immersed in living a real life where actions have consequences that are sometimes significant and sometimes not, but are always remembered.

One of my first projects after we started building the house and barn was a flock of laying hens. They live in my mind still, like one's first love, great white birds shining and perfect in every detail. They roamed by day and put themselves into the chicken house in the evening, and I used to linger outside when I went to close them up and listen to the lullaby sounds of hens settling in for the night. Small talk, feather rustling, feet scraping on the perches as they settled in, the occasional indignant squawk when one pecked another for crowding too close, drowsy comments about the day as they slowly went to rest.

I loved it, and I still do, though my flock now is far more diverse in breed and about half of them roost on a drooping live oak limb just outside the chicken house. The evening sounds are still the same.

I would check the nests anytime I was close to the henhouse, and if I found a few eggs I would slip them into my pockets, always planning to take them to the house. But when you're out and about, things come up unexpectedly. The goats get in the garden, the water tank needs cleaning; somebody is hung in the fence, and so on and so forth. Before I made it to the house, having long since forgotten the eggs in my pockets, calamity would overtake me in the form of a big, enthusiastic dog leaping up on me, a goat muscling its way through a gate and slamming it against me, a bucket loaded with feed smacking into me. The eggs were more often than not scrambled in my pockets.

I just never seemed to learn. It was so easy to grab those eggs and drop them into my pockets, and I made it to the house with whole eggs just enough times to reinforce the belief that it would work.

Many other experiences of our family could be compared to the egg gathering fiascos. There were myriad daily little incursions with the real world that we thought might be worth sharing in a book I intended to call *Eggs in My Pocket*. I just never seemed to get around to putting it all down. Finally, feeling the "empty nest" syndrome, I applied for a stringer's job with *The Williamson County Sun* to write a column covering the Florence/Andice area. It was supposed to be a report of the "news" in those small communities, designed to expand the coverage and thereby the readership of the paper to more of the western parts of the county. Hard news was often in short supply and column inches were often filled with "experiences on the farm." I seldom received comment from anyone other than my editors, most of whom preferred that I become a news reporter and pursue more factual items.

That was until Amy Burroughs filled the editor's chair. She probably recognized that I was not necessarily a news reporter and may have recognized another talent within the columns submitted to her. She called me and asked whether I would like to change the focus of the column to life on the farm. Nothing could have pleased me more, and we discussed a new name for the weekly column. *"Eggs In My Pocket"* was launched, not in the form of a book but in a weekly glimpse of life on a small farm. It's a place where beef comes, not in nice, tidy, impersonal plastic wrapped packages, but in the form of gentle cows with beautiful babies at their sides. Where rain doesn't mean a missed golf game or a weekend outing at the lake cancelled, but whether a crop is going to sprout and mature into feed for the next winter. In that place, sub-freezing temperature doesn't mean placing a couple of logs on the fireplace for a romantic evening, but staying at the barn during the wee small hours to dry off and warm newborn kids to keep them from sickness or death.

For many of my readers who have commented, the columns are a reminder of a yesterday that they remember fondly and enjoy having brought to their consciousness. For some, there are common threads, and it's nice to know that "somebody else thinks that way." For others, the column may represent the opinionated tirades of a cranky granny. For whatever the reasons, *Eggs* has achieved a following, produced many new acquaintances, numerous kind letters to the editor and many encouraging suggestions that "you should put these columns in a book." This book is in response to those many suggestions from my readers.

I hope you enjoy them as much as I enjoyed hearing from you and putting them together.

Eggs In My Pocket

Chapter 1

Life on a Farm Is
Never Dull

Goats are More Like People Than We Realize

Whatever else can be said about life on the farm, nobody can say it's (a) dull or (b) restful, certainly not in the spring. Days are full of trying to get everything done and when its bedtime, usually far later than desirable, you lie down with an uneasy mind, waiting for something to go bump. Well, some of us lie down like that. Papa tends to every emergency with speed and aplomb, but he doesn't waste any of his time worrying about emergencies before they happen, so he falls asleep like dropping a rock into water. I lie listening to the geese clatter and the guineas rattle and the dogs bark, suspecting that the fox is about and when we arise there will be nothing left but feathers on the ground. Experience has taught me that this is not the case, that if I get up and stumble out to look things over, everything will fall suddenly quiet and heads will be tucked under wings before I get there, so unless the racket is unusually raucous, I get a book and read through the din.

There are always exceptions to every rule. One night last week Papa had taken milk I had pasteurized up to the barn for a late feeding of kids and I was cleaning up in the kitchen one last time. He suddenly reappeared and said shortly, "I need your help now! We have a doe in trouble." Couched in those terms, that voice has conditioned me to drop whatever I'm doing and hike it up to the barn. When I got there, he was trying to corner a semi-hysterical Nubian yearling in the dry doe barn. Nubians are born semi-hysterical and perfect their hysteria from there, so that didn't alarm me. She was dodging and turning back like a cutting horse, screaming help! murder! cutthroat! with every other breath. I took a moment to admire her range and power. The peacocks were echoing her alarm in their tree roosts with their trademark help! help!, the chickens were squawking fox! fox! dog! save me! from the barn rafters, and the guineas had just lost it entirely. It takes so little to send a guinea right over the edge at the best of times, but a nighttime crisis is just more than they can collectively handle.

All this is nothing unusual to me; I wasn't freaked until the doe made a sharp turn and I saw her backside. She had started kidding and the baby was not in the proper position, which is nose on outstretched forefeet, like a diver. The first thing you should see in a proper presentation is two little feet; this baby's head was out. No feet, just the whole head. That meant the feet were turned back under the head and the kid was hung and couldn't slide out, as it should. I immediately rethought every aggravated thing I had been thinking about the screaming doe. The really spooky thing was the way the baby was looking around, blinking at the funny new world. Bizarre.

This was actually good; if you don't get a proper presentation, you don't want a tail-first that gets hung, because the umbilical cord will be pinched, the blood supply will fail and the baby will die quickly. This baby needed to be delivered, and fast, but it was perfectly doable if you know how, and Papa does.

Wrestling a screaming, 120-pound yearling that is determined not to go into the nursery stall was not fun; she kept whirling and banging the baby's head against doorframes and gates. The bottle babies had managed to get into the alleyway of the nursery barn and assaulted us in a yelling mob, delighted to see us and demanding milk. I would get two out and three others would flow back in like sand filling up a hole. We had to put two bigger does out to empty a stall for the trying-to-be-new-mother, who by now was wild-eyed and over the top. Bedlam is an understatement. Papa laid the doe down, I leaned on her, talking as fast as I could; it may not have helped her, but I needed reassurance and Papa was far too busy. He found the tiny feet, straightened them out and pulled a pretty baby boy into the world. Pretty, and hungry!

Having been divested of whatever it was that had caused her pain and consternation, the doe was not much inclined to even sniff it, much less feed it. She had to be held while he nursed, which he did like a pro. Full and exhausted from his ordeal, he zonked out. The bottle babies were fed, the mess cleaned up, and we toddled off to bed at about 3:30. I didn't hear geese or anything else for the rest of the dark hours. Next morning, outside the barn, Papa found a tiny black doeling running around hunting mama. She was the firstborn and we had missed her in the dark; she had survived all night with nothing to eat and no mama to look after her. Unfortunately, the doe is indifferent to both of them. They can eat if they're quick, but she apparently has other things on her mind besides raising children.

Goats are sometimes more like people than we realize at first.

Night Life on the Farm

The other night, as I was working up my most persuasive arguments to get Sara started homeward for bath and bedtime after a long reading session; Papa appeared in the bedroom door and said, "Who do you know around here that owns a donkey?"

Running over neighbors in my mind, I asked why and he said, "Because there's one standing in our front yard looking in the windows." Sara squealed in delighted surprise, leaped off the bed where we had been reading and began putting her shoes on with record speed. Grabbing my hand, she dragged me to the door behind Papa, firing questions like, "Is it a baby donkey?" (No) "Do you think Papa will let us keep it?" (This one was a no-brainer, since it belonged to someone already, Papa pointed out with a sigh of relief.)

The dogs were going nuts, but that's such a regular occurrence we hardly notice. What Papa did notice was that the motion lights had tripped and that led to the discovery of the fuzzy gray longears who surveyed us calmly as we tumbled out the front door. He was accompanied by four big yearling calves which Papa quickly recognized as the three black heifers and tiger-striped bull our neighbors had bought about six months ago. They had apparently come home for the holidays.

What followed was reminiscent of an old Laurel and Hardy movie. Papa sent me in to call the folks he thought had bought the calves. I did, and got a very puzzled man on the phone who, when I asked whether he was missing a donkey and four calves, said no, he wasn't, because he didn't own any such animals and I could hear in his voice that he was trying to figure out who the heck I was. Having determined that we had indeed met, except that it was goats instead of calves we had in common, I apologized for disturbing him and went out to ask for another name, preferably the right one this time.

By now the errant visitors were headed down the driveway and there was really no time to call anyone. We piled into the truck and went after them. The heifers were black as the ace of spades; if a car came roaring over the hill it could plow right into them before the driver saw them. We got them into the bar ditch, traveling in the right direction, following the donkey who had apparently decided to go home. We called our son (cell phones can be a good thing) to come block them off at the corner so they would continue to go down the right road, but they would go only so far and then try to turn back, led by one big, black very aggressive heifer. Up and down the road we went, turning them back and trying to keep them from bolting across the road into an unfenced pasture. Once in there, we might not see them again until daylight.

Our daughter appeared, thinking we were after equine escapees again, and was dispatched to the owners' house about a half mile away. They came out immediately, and the donkey went meekly home following the feed bucket. Almost home, the rogue heifer led a stampede into the open acreage and it required spotlights and tramping through brush to flush them out. A cool front blew in while the search raged through the cedars: with Sara wrapped up in a blanket in the truck thoroughly enjoying the chase from our warm vantage point. Two heifers and the bull finally surrendered, but the rogue heifer disappeared into the pitch dark, turning up in our front yard next morning and busting through a fence to rejoin the cows in our pasture. She was ultimately penned and returned home in style via trailer.

Sara was very late to bed, as were we all, but I pointed out that she would have a great story to tell her classmates the next day. She shook her little head, satiny black hair swinging, and said, "Thanks, Gigi, but I don't think they'd believe me."

That's our version of "night life." All it takes is a strange donkey looking in your windows after dark.

Life's Cycle –
The Glad and the Sad

Quite a display the other night, enough thunder and lightning to make one think of April rather than February. All of the resident big hairy cowards were beside themselves long before the storms rolled in heralding more than just a little rain. Sissy, the elder Border collie, has a coat like a polar bear and never opts to come in the house because of cold or heat; she began banging the front door while the rumbles were still faint and the flashes far away. She's sort of an early warning system. There's always time to get things battened down before a storm if you pay attention to Sis.

The peacocks are another excellent alert system. They begin their insistent calling long before one hits. Big birds, they mostly roost as high in trees around the barns as they can get, totally exposed to the elements. A hailstorm would be devastating to them, but only a few of them roost in the barn rafters. The rest of them sit on branches and endure whatever comes their way, screaming about it incessantly.

Everything considered, stormy evenings are pretty rowdy around here. While we had about eight inches of noise and distress, we caught only an inch of rain.

The Ladina cow had her calf a few days ago. That's the cow that knocked me into a brush pile a couple of years ago for daring to approach her new baby too closely, so I always try to be wary when she calves. She's not above an ambush if she thinks you're encroaching on the space she has marked out for herself and her child. This year she has the cutest calf she's ever had. I thought the Jackrabbit Calf was cute last year, with his gray coat and red markings and long ears, but this one is cuter and a heifer to boot, always a plus.

She's a little bitty thing, gray and wrinkly, with a pixie face and a little switchy tail. Her mother is a gigantic black cow with a mottled face and a regal sweep of horns that suggest Longhorn blood somewhere way back. It's funny to see that tiny tyke trailing her big fierce mom, secure in the shadow of the herd boss. They approached the round bale of hay the day after the baby was born, the Ladina cow clearing their way with a few pointed cow comments that caused the other members of the herd to step hastily aside. As she settled in to munch hay the calf lay down under her feet and went to sleep.

Some moms are like that, while others never seem to know exactly what to do with the new little stranger. Children can be such an intrusion on one's routine, especially if you're a herd animal. For mothers like the Ladina cow, though, it's pretty straightforward; there is nothing more important than the child, so one simply bends the environment to fit the immediate need. It works for her.

New babies are the happy side of living closely with animals. The first look around, the first wobbly steps, the amazing delight of that first mouthful of milk; it never gets old. Watching babies turned out with their mothers in the morning, greeting every new day with unbounded enthusiasm and joy, lifts the heart and eases the mind of the watcher. They leap and bounce and pirouette in a dance of sheer exuberance at being alive, their antics a practice of moves they will need as adults, their astonishment at the wonderful world they're born into a constant reminder to us to look around and see what we're looking at rather than just passing by.

There's another side to living with animals that is inevitable and not so happy. I haven't mastered it yet, even after so many years. Babies grow and mature and get old, and they do so at a faster rate than humans do. Regrettably, we all arrive at places we had much rather not go, long before we want to.

A couple of years ago, I bought an old horse. I knew how old he was, and he was thin but not seriously so, and he fattened up pretty fast. He was perfect for me and Grandson Two. He had been around, seen almost everything a horse can see, I guess, and had the scars here and there to prove it. He was unflappable – "bomb-proof", as the horseman's lingo goes, which means he is a solid, sane individual who won't go crazy on you if a plastic bag comes flapping along in the wind.

We named him Sarge. He was sorrel with a white blaze and one white hind foot. That is to say, he was a beautiful reddish brown with a white stripe down his face. His eyes were quiet and kind. He talked to you in the morning and evening at feeding time, his face poking out of his stall as he waited for his senior feed and hay. He loved peppermint treats. The kids could walk under his belly, lead him anywhere, and ride him with a halter. He didn't cost much, but he was worth a lot.

Sarge got sick the other day. Horses don't get sick much, but when they do, you have to do something quick. He had colic, a veterinary term for the bellyache. Some colics are treatable, but some are not. The vet came and did things, but Sarge was old and his colic was bad. He was in a lot of pain and things were just not going to work out. He had come to the end of his string.

Papa and the vet walked him slowly over to the graveyard where there are some other good horses buried. He didn't want to walk, because horses with colic just want to lie down. He always tried to do what you asked him though, so he did. And there, in the gathering dusk, they did the last kind thing they could do for him.

The first thought I had when the storm rolled in the other night was whether Sarge was in the barn, and then I remembered. Grandson Two had gotten up in my lap after it was over and grieved with me, and then said, "Don't worry, Gigi. He was an old horse, and we were good to him. I have some money saved and I'll get you another one. It won't be Sarge, but you'll love it anyway."

Funny how things just seem to go on, no matter what, but I guess I'll wait awhile to take him up on his offer, though.

Sara and Troubles - both about age two.

The Mother of Invention

Living a busy life in town, when a problem arises sometimes the only necessity is finding the phone book and turning to the yellow pages for the number of whatever "professional" is available to fix your problem. There is a great deal to be said for this approach; the older and stiffer I get, the more appealing it is. Of course, like everything else, there are inherent problems even with this solution. The first and most obvious is money, since professionals don't come cheap. The second is time; sometimes the problem might more aptly be termed an emergency, and there isn't a professional in sight. All you get is voice mail or someone telling you there is an opening in his schedule seven weeks from the day you are calling, but there is a waiting list and you will, if you are very, very good, be placed on it.

Around here, we keep baling wire, hay string, nails, screws, bolts, hooks and eyes, scrap lumber, tin, coffee cans (from when coffee came in cans), plastic buckets, old sweatshirts and tee shirts, rubber bands, medicine bottles, glass jars, lids, old garden hose, pvc pipe in every size, chain, boxes, feed sacks, plastic bags, ad infinitum. Yet we often need something we don't have. The one thing never lacking is Papa's boundless supply of imaginative approaches to whatever crisis arises. True, sometimes he does have to give in and go to the hardware store –preferably a real one like the one in Florence, which is a genre rapidly disappearing from the scene, much to the detriment of our society – but even then he employs his ingenuity to solve the current dilemma.

It's that quality that seems to be sadly lacking in most men I meet who are under the age of, say, fifty, and even a good many men who are older.

If it doesn't come prepackaged, hanging on an s-hook in a big box store replete with a 31-page instruction book, they don't know what to do with it and want no part of it. Some of them don't want any part of it under any circumstances, preferring to get on the aforementioned waiting list, and that certainly is their choice, but everyone involved misses out on a lot. The man doesn't have the mental exercise of assessing the problem, figuring out the solution and implementing it, complete with pride of accomplishment. If there is a spouse, she doesn't get to "gofer" the essential roll of duct tape or plumber's cement and hold things, such as flashlights and sharp cutting tools, while her husband works. Kids don't get to see dad do much besides punch numbers into a phone to summon someone to "fix it". Of course, they miss out on some colorful language they will later go into time out for using themselves, but isn't that part of growing up?

This is a generalization, of course; there are plenty of inventive men and women out there whom I will never meet who are taking care of business themselves, but there are plenty who don't. I truly believe the frustration of wading through the red tape of getting a simple problem resolved by an "official" repairman who won't "void the warranty" is much more harmful to a person than sitting down and problem solving on his own.

The most recent example of problem solving on the cheap and simple involved a big brown Nubian doe and Papa. Somehow the doe broke her foreleg during the night. Nubians can be notorious schizophrenics, so who knows how she managed it, but it is a bad break. Papa splinted it and gave her the appropriate antibiotic shots and she was placed in a deeply bedded stall to heal. Except she didn't. She wouldn't even try to get up, so Papa fashioned a sling out of a plastic feed sack and some hay twine and twice a day he suspended her from the rafters so that her feet just touched the ground, hoping to keep her circulation good. He redid the splint and things didn't look good. After a month he discovered that she had developed an infection in the leg and also a dreadful sore under her belly, just in front of the udder. Decision time.

By this time she was getting up on her own, but the infection was not good. A vet visit confirmed what we feared and aggressive treatment was prescribed. "Keep the belly wound clean," the vet said. She squinted at the recumbent doe who was greedily searching Sara's hands for more animal cookies and said thoughtfully, "Try putting some big old shorts on her to keep the bedding out of the wound and the medicine on it".

It may not have been what the vet had in mind exactly, but Papa dredged up a pair of stretched out jockey shorts from his rag box in the shop and we got the doe into them. She wore a totally confused expression along with the shorts, and by the next morning she had divested herself of them entirely. That's when Papa had his flash of genius, told me what to get, and we rigged her up that evening. I was at the vet's the next day with a new rescue dog and she asked about the doe. I described the fiasco of the shorts, but told her that Papa had solved it. Leaning across the exam table she said with a grin, "What did he do, put suspenders on her?"

Great minds run in the same channel, I guess, because that's exactly what he did and it's working out swell.

Now where did I put that camera....

The Signs Just Have To Be Right

She's done it again. The foolish peach tree down in the orchard is blooming like crazy, just like she always does every spring. The other trees around her are loaded with round green buds just waiting for a few warm, sunny days to bring them around, but that foolish tree never can contain herself. Granted, she is an early peach, but there's early and then there's early.

It's not like she's a juvenile who doesn't know any better. She's been in the ground for at least ten or twelve years, and I can't remember a year when she didn't jump the gun and pop blossoms long before anything else was blooming. She has brightened many a gray day with her rosy cloud of blossoms. Every year I've thought she would freeze and bear no fruit, but every year she has proven me wrong. Her branches are as loaded with sweet juicy peaches as any of her orchard mates who bloom much later.

I'm so fond of that silly tree that I wrote a poem inspired by her.

An Upstart Plum Tree

That upstart plum tree bloomed again.
Snow all around, hip high on a tall man,
Deep blue nights crackling with cold,
But no matter! Two bright days,
Mild sunkisses, soft southern breeze stroke
And she pops, shameless.
She floats above the snow, whiter still,
A cloud of dazzle, scent sharper for the biting air,
Incandescent in the purple winter evening.
Her petals drift, settle on the crust, white shadows.
She never sets a plum, that foolish thing,
Always too early in her blooming,
But how she fills the heart!

A whole new gardening season beckons, and sitting down with a hot cup of something and the seed catalogs sends the imagination soaring. Ambition expands and increases the garden. This year we should put in an asparagus bed, and maybe try Brussels sprouts again. Most importantly, this will surely be the Year of the Perfect Tomato. Oh, for big, red, warm tomatoes sitting heavy in my hand!

That's how it all looks now, bundled into a sweater and heavy socks and sitting with my feet on the hearth. However, when July afternoons hit the triple digits and the whole world wilts under the furnace blast of the summer sun, enthusiasm wilts accordingly. The Perfect Tomato morphs into a project for the fall garden and it becomes a chore just to keep things alive until the weather cools off.

Why is it that in February, planning the garden, all things seem possible, but in July it just seems like a lot of sweaty work? There's the heat, of course, but it's more than that. There are only so many ways to fix zucchini before you have to admit that you don't really like the stuff all that much to begin with, and while the 97th tomato is likely just as good as the first...somehow it isn't.

Still, it's always fun, the planning. Part of that planning is checking the signs for the best days to plant. Papa scoffs at the whole idea, even though his farmer grandfather was scrupulous in his attention to the signs with regard to planting, butchering, weeding and whatever else had to be done on the farm. Papa says the signs are right when you have time to get the plants into the ground, but I know better.

I once read to him out of *The Foxfire Book* how to set fence posts so they would stay in the ground straight and solid. It had to be done in a certain phase of the moon. He went out and found the most crooked cedar tree he could and made a fence post out of it. I saw him set a straight post, and the next day he called me to come look at the new post. It was crooked as a dog's hind leg. He said the moon just pulled it right over and twisted it up, and he had me going for quite awhile. Of course, he had dug up the straight post and replaced it with the crooked one, just to razz me about my "signs".

Seemed like a lot of trouble to prove a point. I told him if he'd left the crooked one in the ground, maybe the moon would have straightened it out for him.

Chapter 2

Some Days Are
More Special Than
Others

New Year's Resolutions

New Year's resolutions are easy to make. All it takes is the right setting, the right frame of mind, and maybe a stomachache from too much rich food. Losing weight in the coming year is probably the most common resolution we make, followed by a vow to exercise, exercise and exercise. Many of us actually begin the New Year with the new program in a veritable fit of enthusiasm and determination, resolved that this time we will follow it through to its happy – and lighter – conclusion.

By February our busy schedule has reasserted itself and all the bad old habits have crept back into our lives. Guilt and the all too frequent chocolate bar have supplanted resolution, and things are pretty much the same. This does not apply to all those hardy souls who routinely arise at dawn, don their jogging togs, and hit the road as a matter of course. Those guys are easily recognizable; they wear sweats that have seen better days, running shoes that were obviously made for running, hair swept up under a cap or tied back, and a pleasantly serious expression. They are usually actually sweating.

These are the same slim, trim folks who will tell you that they experience "runner's high", a fable, in my opinion, and that they don't feel well if they don't exercise every day. They obviously need more chocolate in their lives.

But they never have to make stupid resolutions at the turning of the year, because they haven't had eggnog and peanut brittle and more carbs at every meal than they usually consume in a week.

My resolution in that regard is to do the best I can to stay where I am, since budging pounds seems to be pretty much impossible for me. Along with that I can try to eat more sensibly and move the whole thing more, but I don't plan to beat myself up if I can't measure up to society's ideal of "the mature woman". That image bears little resemblance to most of the "mature women" I know. I am now a "woman of a certain age"; my youth is past and cannot be recaptured, no matter how much diet, exercise, and surgery I might undergo. Healthier I might be; younger, never.

Smarter? I like to think so. We older citizens are smarter in many ways, aren't we, just by the process of living? We know certain basic things by instinct now, such as, if you run a red light on 2338 you stand a very good chance of acquiring a. a ticket, b. the animosity of about 237 drivers with whom you just shared the intersection, or c. a body cast, six months' worth of rehab and at least one lawsuit resulting from the multi-car wreck you caused. And that's if you're lucky.

But are we smart enough to have truly benefited by all those days and nights of life? Do we realize how we impact the world every single day just by how we move in it? And do we recognize how much room for improvement there is in every single one of us?

Sometimes, at odd times, I see how much better I could be, how much kinder, more patient, more lenient in my judgments of those around me I should be. So this year, weighty issues aside, I have a set of resolutions all my own.

I will try to see when I look, whether it is at the dwindling patches of still-lovely countryside, the animals I care for, the night sky, someone's eyes or the faces of my grandchildren and the other people I love. I will try to understand the motives behind the behavior of people I interact with and, indeed, every being right down to the pesky, birdseed-thieving squirrels in the backyard. I will try to hear when I listen, not just to the words, but also to the real meaning behind them, especially with children, who so often are not listened to at all, and the very elderly, who have come full circle and once again are invisible.

I can't promise to love everybody, but I sure will try to love the people I do love a whole lot better. That means I will try most of all not to leap to conclusions and make judgments and issue opinions without at least a little bit of thought before I speak. I will try to be kind.

Perhaps I won't do any better at all that than I have done at losing weight in the past, but it's worth a try.

Happy New Year!

A Word or Two On Love

Since it's almost Valentine's Day a word on love seems appropriate. While Valentine's Day has less to do with love than with retail sales, still it's a day dedicated to the contemplation and expression of romantic love. As a subject of song, story, fable and rhyme, love has no equal unless it's war. Wars have been fought for love of one kind or another; Helen of Troy, Romeo and Juliet, Hamlet, all driven by different forms of love. The Beatles sang "All you need is love", and they believed it, just like all hopeful young things believe it. So did I, and so did you, probably. We learn, alas, that it helps to have a bit more than that, but love in some form is essential to all of us. Newborn babies abandoned in a hospital die for the lack of it and thrive when volunteers hold and cuddle them every day. Old people long for that same expression of affection, lost to them over the years.

When I was 15 I had my first "real" boyfriend, indeed the only one I ever had except the one I have been married to for 49 years. I shared my first kiss with him and it's true, you never forget it. Brief and chaste but absolutely electric – this was the early '50's, you know – it just made me giddy. He didn't have any money, but he carved me a wooden horse because he knew I was horse crazy. It was pretty ugly, I guess, but I cherished it until I lost it in our house fire. It said to me better than any fancy gift, that he knew who I was and what mattered to me, and that's rare at any age.

Young love like that is sappy, isn't it, but sweet with a sweetness that can't last. Hanging on the phone for hours just listening to each other breathe, after you've just been together for hours before that, with really nothing to say that you haven't said a hundred times already. Your folks are yelling at you to get off the phone right now, but you just can't bear to break the connection. One of you goes on vacation for a week and the one left behind suffers agonies; you can't eat, sleep or think until your beloved gets back. And if one of you looks at somebody else with more than passing interest, it's awful; it's the end of life as the spurned one knows it. You can't possibly live without him/her.

Sure you can. We grow up, hopefully, and learn who we are ourselves so that we can learn how to be half of a couple and do it well. From the first flush of romantic love when everything either one of you does is pure magic, to that morning when you wake up and look at each other and think "whatever made me think this was a good idea?", to the day when you look at each other and think, "I'm really glad we're still together," it's an evolving process. In that process we learn a little about the different kinds of love.

There's the love expressed when he brings you flowers or chocolates and you don't even mind when he eats most of them because he's so wonderful and you love to watch him chew. Later there's the love you're so grateful for when he gets up at 3 a.m. and feeds and changes the baby when you think you'll die if you have to do it again. Raising kids through teen years brings out a special kind of love, the kind with stamina and teeth in it. Still later there's the love you couldn't make it without when you get a diagnosis nobody wants and he says, it'll be okay, we'll be okay. Mixed in there somewhere is the love you hang onto grimly when he's done something really stupid or you cross a line you've never crossed before and things are tightlipped and grim for a while.

Papa used to give me a potted rose on Valentine's Day, and it's a mark of the kind of love he has that he also planted the rose and almost always where I wanted it to go. After all this time I have learned what's really important to me and it isn't jewelry or cruises in the Caribbean. I want someone who understands what's happening and what I need to get through it. When Sarge, my old gelding, had his last bout of colic and had to be put down, Papa helped the vet and then buried Sarge and didn't make me go through any more than I had to. When my dogs die, he will reassure me that I have not been selfish and neglectful, thereby causing the demise of 17-year-old friends, and will bury them gently and respectfully for me. He never tells me I can't, but almost always tells me sure I can, and then helps me any way he can, no matter what I'm trying. Two dozen roses one day of the year is no match for the steadiness of that kind of love.

He leaves cabinet doors open; he makes terrible messes and walks away to start a new project; the office is a wreck and while he can find a tiny scrap of paper in all that mess, he can't find his socks. But he plays basketball with Sara almost every night out on the driveway, and he reads with Grandson Two with infinite patience and shows Grandson One how to do a project in the shop. He lets me sleep in the morning sometimes when I know he doesn't want me to.

I think I'll keep him, at least until after our 50th anniversary.

It's kind of sappy, maybe, but it feels pretty darned good to me. Happy Valentine's Day.

How Do We Spell Love?

Easter weekend is upon us, with all its religious significance and secular events. There is often a great deal of argument over which has the major influence over the holiday, and I couldn't begin to discuss all that. It's much easier to observe and enjoy all aspects of Easter in their turn.

As a time of rebirth and rejuvenation, Easter has no equal. It's fitting that it happens in the spring, since renewal of life is the most prevalent occurrence on the farm just now. The barn is full of new kids and the pastures with new calves. Baby chicks scurry after mama hens and hens are broody in the most unlikely places. The workload doubles and triples with the advent of babies, but what joy they always bring! Without them, what would be the point of having the farm?

Grandsons One and Two and Sara have been helping in the garden; they love to dig anywhere, especially freshly tilled ground, and they will fetch and carry a bit less enthusiastically. Let one of them get hold of a garden hose and the fun really begins, waxing as the actual planting wanes. Sometimes you have so much help you just give up for the time being, but how dull it would seem if they weren't there.

Easter is intended to remind us of love, and that, too, lies in abundance around us. New mama does talk to their babies in a special voice, unmistakable once you've heard it, encouraging them to gain their feet and nurse, welcoming them to the world. The voice changes in a few days to a more normal tone, but still they watch and protect and encourage their little ones. Cows do the same, a bit less energetically as a rule, but no less intensely. Seeing a cow charge a dog who has gotten too close to her calf leaves no doubt in your mind as to the devotion they afford their offspring.

Perhaps one of the fiercest expressions of love can be found in a really good mama hen. I have a couple of bruises from pecks delivered by an Auraucana hen recently in defense of her nest. She didn't just peck; she grabbed a piece of skin and twisted it. Such a hen's eyes glitter with determination; if she had a chin it would be firmly set. This one fluffs to three times her size when I just approach her nest, and her babies are still in the egg. I would wager she will raise them all, natural dangers notwithstanding, unless I get brave enough to grab her up and cage her before the eggs hatch. She has maternal zeal to the nth degree.

Here I would offer a plea; don't buy little colored chickens for your children or grandchildren. Not only do they come in the most outlandish colors Nature never intended, they are fragile. They can be easily loved to death by warm, well-meaning little hands. They need lots of care; heat, feed, water, protection. They grow up to be roosters, for the most part, if they grow up at all, and roosters crow. A lot. I like it, but neighbors may not. Confined, they need daily care. Unconfined, you may be sorry. They scratch in the flowerbeds, poop on the porch, and are a general nuisance. Once they are scraggly teenaged roosters, the fluffy baby look long gone, what do you do with them? It's not cool to eat Alfred.

The same thing goes for baby ducks, only more so. Ditto baby bunnies. It's like getting that adorable big-footed, soulful-eyed pup that grows up to weigh 90 pounds and chews up the scenery because he has to live alone in the yard all the time because everybody is busy. The shelters are full of them, condemned through no fault of their own. Don't do it. Get a cuddly stuffed animal that won't suffer when its time in the spotlight is over and it's relegated to the toy basket. Ultimately you'll be so glad you did.

Easter is about joy and love. To make that last takes effort and dedication and a little bit of forethought.

Sara's preschool had their egg hunt and she was up for it. Nowadays they specify what the plastic eggs can contain; no chocolate (it melts), no unwrapped candy, etc. Sara loaded hers with stickers and gum and a quarter. She's very big on quarters, since it takes a quarter to get a gumball or a handful of little colored gum from the machines. She quite possibly believes that every quarter minted has her name on it, so adding a quarter to the eggs she filled was a genuine gesture of love for "her kids".

She went off with her Easter basket and sporting a new outfit; a shirt with "Ladybug" on the front and long-legged little jeans with ladybugs embroidered down the sides. A red cap with a big ladybug perched on her silky black hair and let me tell you, if there was a cuter kid anywhere in the world, I couldn't have stood the sight. Ladybug has been one of her nicknames since she was tiny.

Talk about joy and love – you spell that Sara.

Red, White and Blue

Upon us already, the 4th of July, parades and flags and fireworks combine with speeches and patriotic music and lots of traditional food to make one of our most meaningful and important celebrations. Never mind the "fireworks sale" and the "hottest summer sale" fliers that advertise all the great bargains the chain stores have waiting for you on this weekend. That's not what it's about. It's the most uniquely American holiday going, about celebrating who we are and how we got here. Imperfect though it all may be, it's still the best game in town, and we're the best at playing it.

With summer less than three weeks old it feels like late July or worse, we've had no rain, pastures browned and dry and the garden shot. The perfect tomato will just have to wait for a better year. Summers like this leave us dreaming of mountains where it rains every day, the nights are crisp and the mornings deliciously sweatshirt cool. Snowmelt streams rushing down slopes with a warbling sound, fresh wind off the mountaintops still frosted with snow, birds and little creatures rushing around, all that sounds nice.

Instead, I live among blasted pastures with cracks in the ground big enough to drop a squirrel into; the wind, if any, will chap your lips and blister your face, and the birds sit on branches among wilting leaves with their beaks open, waiting for the little bit of cooling we get in the evening. During the day the cows and horses stand or lie in the shade, expending no energy to move around. The goats find the breeziest spot on the farm and spend the afternoon there. My big hairy cowards pass the hours under the air-conditioning, and when I invite them to go out they eye me suspiciously, as if to say, "Are you going out there? Do we get to come right back in? What's the catch?"

Only cats never seem to get especially hot. Ever notice that? Cats are just cool. They don't do much, true, but they seldom pant and they always appear smooth and unruffled when the rest of us are gasping and sweaty, hair plastered to our heads and clothes all akimbo, completely out of sorts.

There is a wren's nest on Grandson Two and Sara's garage that Papa is watching; the little pair has four babies and they both keep up a continuous food train, dumping fat white larvae and bugs and who knows what into four perpetually gaping maws that open the second a parent appears. Papa feels sorry for them. He says they're so little, and they work so hard, he wishes he had something to set out for them to feed the youngsters.

One thing we can all do is provide water for small creatures in this perishing dry time. We leave a drip at the water tanks, but I also put out old pie tins or other shallow dishes in tucked-away places for the frogs and small things. Almost every dog bucket or small duck dish I turn out to clean sports a frog floating in it; they hop in, driven by thirst and dry skin, but they can't hop out. They need their own dishes. Birds need lots of water, too, but be sure it's not on the ground where an enterprising cat can make an ambush. I love to watch the birds enjoy a sprinkler if it washes over low hanging tree branches; they sing and preen and bathe to our heart's delight.

Other than trying to keep everything watered, all I can do is hope for rain and think as hard as I can of October, though even if all of Texas thought of it together, October won't come one day sooner. "Don't wish time away," my granma used to say, and I don't. Just heat and drought. That's allowed.

The Good Kind of Scared

It's almost the end of October, but it feels like the middle of May. Every time I step out the door I get wet, and the pastures are still green. I almost expect the peach trees to bloom any day; they haven't much sense about season, it seems, and when it's warm and wet for long enough, they pop. Rain is good; we aren't allowed to complain about rain, as I've mentioned before. But I can – and do – complain about mud!

Rubber boots are a way of life in weather like this. Pairs of boots in every size from Sara to Papa stand guard outside the back door, ready to go to the barn or the pasture. There is only one problem about boots, for me at least. Spiders can take up residence in boots that haven't been worn in awhile. When I peer down into the depths of a boot and see cobwebs, I'm not real anxious to stick my foot in there. Or my hand, either. I've been known to get the shop vac and suck everything that I don't think should be in there, out. Papa just turns his upside down, gives them a shake or two, and rams his foot in. I wince.

You can't do without boots on a farm, but they do have their limitations. In really rainy years, I've been in mud deeper than my boots were tall. One of the ickiest feelings in the world is cold mud sliding down inside your boot. You can't do a thing about it but just go on shooing cows or carrying hay or whatever you were doing, with mud sloshing around inside your boot.

Once we were sorting cows in the lot and, as usual, Papa was directing me where to go to achieve the desired effect. The lot was full of aggravated 1000-pound cows with their lightning quick calves, not one of which wanted to go where Papa wanted them to. I had no real desire to be dumped into the soupy mess underfoot by a cranky cow, but even walking was a chore. Turning, dodging and evading was out of the question. Stranded in the middle of the lot, surrounded by big muddy bovines churning up the slew even more, I felt the mud grab my boot and suck it right off my foot. Now I am standing on one leg, balancing the socked foot on my calf and trying to reach the boot firmly mired in the muck.

Papa is exasperated, to say the least. I am running out of options fast and the cows don't give a hoot about anything but getting out of the lot. A Kodak moment...or is that Prozac?

What happened? Well, I'm not a screamer, so I went down pretty quietly. It wasn't pretty, but it all worked out. Papa opened the gate and nobody stepped on me. We sorted cows another, drier day, I think.

The mud isn't that bad yet this year, but there sure are lots of muddy paw prints everywhere. The dogs don't wear boots, and they don't mind mud.

It's almost Halloween, and I don't know about your house, but around here it's pretty close to the best holiday of the year. Kids love to be scared. Not really scared; thank goodness most of our kids never know true terror and we don't want them to. Just shivery, giggly, grab on to somebody and squeal scared. The kind of scared they get when a big tall uncle grabs them from behind, turns them upside down and jiggles the daylights out of them. Good kind of scared.

Halloween plays right into that. Ghosts and goblins and black cats and bats and witches with tall pointy hats, all symbols of a deliciously spooky evening. The boys have always gotten into it with gusto, even when they were small. Trick or treat is a big deal; you'd think they never saw candy at any other time of the year. They used to go door to door, followed by parents and grandparents with cameras recording how cute they were and reminding them to say thank you, and after every foray they would open their bags and compare notes, gauging their own and the other fellow's haul.

They never hesitated to go to a door, even when the porch was decorated with fake spider webs and spooky music, and though they might back up a bit if a witch or monster opened the door, they recovered, bravely declaring "trick or treat!" and holding up their bags. Then they ran away, giggling, chattering about what they had seen, on to the next conquest. Once home, they poured everything out in piles on the floor, each child going through the goodies like a sultan sifting jewels through his fingers. The most desirable treats went into one pile, the next choice into another, and the stuff they didn't want got handed over to somebody else. There wasn't usually much of that.

For a couple of weeks they delved into their stash, sifting and sorting and gauging how long it would last. They are turning nine this weekend, one of them the day before Halloween and one the day after. Things are a bit more circumspect now, a bit more restrained. They still plan a big evening, complete with costumes, and you can see the sparkle of anticipation in their eyes, but if you bring it up they're cool. I miss the little towheads dancing up the sidewalks, too full of excitement to walk and just a little bit deliciously scared of what waits behind the next door.

But there is still Sara. Sara has always reacted to things in a polar opposite fashion to the boys. She hates the Fourth of July as much as my dogs do. Trying to get her to look at the beautiful colors in the fireworks displays doesn't work because she has her hands on her ears and is screaming, "Too loud! Too loud! I hate it!" She will hardly watch from inside the house as the boys (big and little) shoot off their carefully planned and ever more intricate displays of explosives, the louder and bigger the better.

Sara likes to be a little scared. Very little. She determines the degree. Little kids she knows in kitty costumes and princess dresses and monster face paint pass muster. Bigger kids in ghoulish getups send her into someone's arms where she buries her head and says, "I want to go home now!" This year she is a black cat, complete with face mask which none of us expect her to wear. She is, of course, adorable. Last year her little face framed in straight black hair and punctuated by big dark eyes won smiles at every house she visited. Her shy smile and soft "thank you" usually resulted in an extra piece of candy dropped into her sack. The boys watched incredulously as she garnered goodies at a rate twice that of their own. Papa laughed at their complaints.

"Get used to it, guys," he told them. "She's got something you guys will never have." When they pressed him to explain, he just smiled and told them they'd understand someday. Which of course they will.

Still, Sara has reservations about Halloween. It will be very dark, the people will be strangers, and she isn't so sure about ringing doorbells. "I like the candy part," she explained earnestly the other day, "but I can do without the scary part."

Isn't that a lot like life in general? We all like the candy part, but we could do without the scary part, for sure. Happy Halloween!

Trick or Treat

Thanksgiving Opens the Door

So, we did it all again, the Thanksgiving thing. It was different this year, but interesting. Every grandchild had a Thanksgiving dinner at his/her school, and we went. Pretty good food and the company was the best part. Being still in pre-school, Sara had made a costume to wear. The kids got to choose what they wanted to be, Pilgrims or Indians. (Please, I know from Native Americans, but these guys were Indians!) Some of the little girls wore doily caps pinned in their hair, or Pilgrim hats with ruffled collars. Sara and most of the little boys had feathered headbands and vests cut from brown paper bags, colored as brightly as crayons could make them. She also sported a necklace made of Fruit Loops strung on brown twine, and we thought she was absolutely fetching.

My scant knowledge of the history of the Pilgrim Fathers makes me think it would be lots more fun to be an Indian than a Pilgrim. Not that Indians had it so easy, but Pilgrim life sounds fairly grim, what with the stocks and dunking stools and all. I imagine the Indian guests at that first Thanksgiving were mostly thankful they weren't Pilgrims. They didn't wear tight shoes that hurt their feet, or layers of clothes that restricted their movement, and they lived a natural life. I'm pretty sure the Pilgrim Fathers were against living a natural life.

The whole Thanksgiving thing got me thinking about how wonderful and strange life is, and how little we appreciate it. I saw the title of an article on the cover of a magazine while waiting in the impossible line in the grocery store and it made me laugh out loud. And then I felt really bad.

"Do Your Best On Not Enough Rest", it said. What? Isn't that an oxymoron?

It's funny, but lots of people seem to be against living a natural life. They don't mean to be, but they are. There are so many things that get in the way of doing what feels right; it's easy to lose the reality in the clamor of the moment and our own uncertainty. We are so impatient. We don't have time to wait for things to work out. You've got to get with the program or get left behind.

Good. It's more comfortable back here with the misfits, the oddballs, the different ones. If you're not in such a hurry, you can watch the cattle giving thanks for sunshine after two weeks of dreary sodden days, and hear the hens prattle on about how rain really brings out the earthworms and oops! there's a good one! You can take note of Albert, the cat who fancies himself a mighty hunter, back in hot pursuit of insolent squirrels he will never catch, and you are too kind to point out to him that he is pathetic at hunting and should stick to cat food.

You would have seen the first clear sunset after many days of rain, the sky all yellow and gold and blazing red on the horizon, and the dark blue bowl of the cloudless sky overhead. You could have smelled Canada on the sharp north wind when you faced into it. Well, maybe not Canada, but someplace exotic, like Seattle.

You would have swung somebody in a swing, just because she asked you to, and the way she laughed when she went especially high would be music in your heart.

I am thankful to be a misfit, to have the chance to live as much of a natural life as I can. I don't want to haul the deer off in special trailers to be slaughtered because they eat my plants or get in the way of my golf cart. Feeding them to the homeless doesn't make it feel any more right to me. I haven't the right to decide the fate of wild creatures based on my self-interest.

Nor do I believe a natural life is easy and charming. It can be grim and heartbreaking. But it belongs to you in a way the artificially contrived life never can.

We are coming up on the birthday of one of the most natural men who ever lived. Thanksgiving opens the door to that more spiritual celebration.

Breathe Deep and Have a Cup of Tea

It's all done by now. Christmas, that is. Gifts are bought, wrapped and maybe given. Santa has made his annual sweep, to the delight of children lucky enough to have a visit from him. Lights are glowing, music playing, turkey roasting – or frying – people gathered together to enjoy the day. Just for a little while we try to forget the sorrows and worries of every other day and be in the moment joyous.

Sometimes it actually happens. Everybody is healthy and well and in a good humor. Nobody's coughing or running fever, and nobody has so much as a headache. Nobody makes a major gaffe or deliberately incites a riot by an inflammatory remark or begins to cry for no reason. Gifts please, affections rise, old enmities do not, laughter abounds, dinner is pleasantly consumed and just for a little while the world balances on perfect harmony.

Now, of all times, peace and harmony are most appropriate. Other gatherings may resemble the Gunfight at the OK Corral more than a family birthday party, but Christmas at least should be happy. Aunt Hazel brought that jello thing again and her first remark to you was about the newest five pounds you already knew you had put on, but so what? Uncle Elbert laughs too loud, but the kids are all congregated around him, rolling on the floor at his really corny jokes, and he's glowing in the midst of his audience. There are no less than five green bean casseroles, but they all seem to have been made from different recipes and anyway, green beans are good for you. Cousin Alice's kids are not one bit better behaved than they were last year, but they're no worse, either. Your small kingdom is cleaned and decorated and the smell of Christmas candles mingles with the smells of Christmas cooking to create an olfactory delight all through the house, in spite of what your significant other thinks. He's never cared for perfume of any kind, but he graciously has done nothing other than wrinkle his nose at you a time or two. All is well.

I speak of real families here, not the families who appear in the Christmas letters you find in many cards you receive. If you find it hard to recognize those people, it's because they don't exist. According to many of those epistles, life is one long round of adventurous success. The children are exhaustingly overachieving virtuosos of virtually every super strenuous sport available to them, meanwhile maintaining a grade average so high that there is no true measurement for it. The parents are doing so well on every level – personal, financial, spiritual – that they should be embarrassed to admit it. Unfortunately, they are not. As the recipient of such letters, instantly measuring your own probably quite plain and humdrum life – read "normal" - against the gleaming pinnacle of happiness and solvency, you must make a quick decision. Do you soldier on like most of the world, wondering why the heck the kid can't get math even with a tutor and how to manage ever increasing taxes on an ever shrinking budget, or do you just check your will for people you've decided to leave out and open a vein?

Relax. Breathe deeply. Have a cup of tea or take a walk. Get a grip. There is room for all of us in the world, especially at this most blessed and forgiving season. Send out your own letter and give the overachievers something to really feel good about. "This year has been a little rough, but we expect little Kestrel will do better at the alternative school this term. We hope so, since three years in sixth grade is probably enough, and, incidentally, that thing with the knife was kind of over-reported in the media and we understand no one involved will need plastic surgery after all. We did find Granny in Vegas, though we have no idea how she got there, and she won $600 during her stay. Of course, her bail was a little more than that, but she had a good time, I guess. Jefferson hopes to find another job as soon as he can locate a boss who understands that he just cannot show up every single day. Don't you agree that's a tad unreasonable, especially for a man of his talent and ability? As for me, the voices are much less a distraction since I started the new meds. I do sleep a lot, but it keeps me out of trouble."

As for my merry little band, we are together and more or less pleased about it, struggling to love one another in spite of, not because of. In this season of love and light, I wish there was more happiness and harmony in the world, less anger and pain and misunderstanding, not just now, but every day. All any of us can do is the best we can, right where we are. Smile at somebody when you really would like to smack him/her, because that's probably when he/she needs a smile the most. Think before you take offense; maybe you won't need to. Listen, listen, listen. Few of us are really good at that. Don't ask, "How are you?" unless you really want to know. Lots of little kindnesses roll through the year into one big ball of caring and support almost without your noticing, but it won't go unrewarded. You'll have this warm spot inside that makes you feel good, even when you get those Christmas letters.

Chapter 3

Birds of a Feather

The Don Juan of the Chicken World

Spring is hatching time. Geese, ducks, guineas and chickens set nests of eggs and turn them into babies with their fierce maternal heat. Peacocks set a bit later, always out in the boonies where humans seldom find them but foxes always can. Game chickens, of course are an exception; those hardy, feisty little hens know no season. They hatch in the dead of winter if the broody mood takes them, and I'll swear they can set on a box of rocks and turn them into chicks. For the most part, though, feathered babies emerge from the egg in spring.

This spring we have the usual assortment of chicks lodged in cages with their mothers after having been gathered up out of the goat pens and horse stalls where the hens chose to nest. One little gold hen has a brood of fifteen fluff balls and she is no friend of mine; when I opened the cage to renew their food and water, she rushed screaming at my offending arm and flogged me soundly. She's over the top with the mother thing. Another, little white hen, has about a dozen but she is far less intensely involved. One has the feeling that if the fox took one or two she might hardly notice. The rest of the hens are in between with regard to their offspring.

We have four goslings this year, and if there are birdlings cuter than these I don't want to see them. When they were hours out of the egg, foofy little yellow fluff balls toddling around the pen with their parents, Papa set a shallow pan of water in the pen with a brick in the middle so that the babies could get out when they got tired, and we stood back to watch. Within minutes they were in the water, swimming deliriously about, ducking their tiny heads under and coming up to preen their baby bodies in an enchanting imitation of the big handsome birds watching them so proudly. How did they know to do that? They had never seen water or big birds swimming; they had barely seen the light of day. But they knew exactly what to do, and what's more, they love doing it.

The rest of the flock gathered round the cage, discussing the children at length and at the top of their voices while the parent birds hovered near the babies, joining in the conversation occasionally. We always have to put the gander in with the goose and goslings. He has guarded them faithfully while they were in the nest, and he will not stand for being separated from them once they hatch. When the goslings are big enough to be turned out, the whole flock will take on the responsibility of their care; they never heard of Hillary, but they know it takes a village to raise a child.

Chickens, on the other hand, are the masters of the single-parent family, and that parent is always the mom. Dad forgot about the whole thing roughly 30 seconds after it happened – that is, until the next time – and the only attention a rooster gives chicks is to peck them if they get in his way. I have a big dark red rooster with sapphire green tail feathers; his name is Errol Flynn. He is gorgeous and he knows it, spending most of his time posing and pecking at the ground, lying to the hens that he has found a choice bug under this leaf and will be glad to share. He will do nothing of the sort, using the bug line to reel in the unsuspecting hens, who inevitably fall for it and are pounced upon by that Don Juan of the chicken world, the ever-lecherous Errol. His sons, incidentally, follow in his footsteps.

Guineas are so scattered I'm not sure how the whole thing happens. I see them running back and forth like mad things with first one chasing and then, after a scrambling turnabout, the chasee becoming the chaser, but I've never actually seen one catch another one, and certainly I've never found a nest. Frankly, I can't picture a guinea hen setting a nest since that would require holding relatively still for some time, and I've never seen one do that, either. I have seen hens with a clutch of babies trying vainly to keep up with their addlepated mother, and have raised them under a lamp. They turn out just as jangled and brainless as their elders. This year Papa found a nest and put eggs under a game hen, who immediately took on the task of turning eggs into babies. She happily hatched close to a dozen, and it would be lovely if she could have given them even a bit of her chicken sense, but I fear when they leave the shelter of her wings they will go chittering off in ten directions at once, hopelessly guinea. I love guineas in spite of themselves, but I have no illusions about them. They are witless wonders, amazing at keeping grasshoppers and other bugs under control and death on snakes. I guess it's okay to be a hysterical fruitloop if you are very good at what you do.

Peahens wear their dignity even onto a nest, setting eggs with an air of hauteur and a slightly bored expression, their long bodies settled deep into the hay and tails stretched out behind. Even when you approach to count the eggs they maintain a faintly disdainful distance with their eyes, seeming neither alarmed nor interested. Newly hatched babies wear that same expression, miniaturized, their tiny heads crowned with a Roman riff of almost invisible feathers. They are unmistakably royalty among the barnyard set and move among the other fowl with measured step and haughty air, but the truth is they aren't long on brains. After all, they sit in the tops of dead trees and scream bloody murder when a storm approaches instead of roosting in the rafters of the barn.

Come to think of it, I know people who can't seem to avoid one train wreck after another in their lives, so I guess we're not so different after all. It's all in the way you look at it.

He's all that – he thinks!

Beauty Often Tends to Blind Us to the Brain Size

There is possibly nothing in nature as beautiful as a mature male peacock. He takes the eye instantly and the human observer almost always makes an ooooh sound. When a big male is sitting atop a fence post with his iridescent indigo neck stretched out and his tail nearly dragging the ground, exuding self-importance and haughty grandeur, watchers are often too impressed to say anything. Ah, but when he really struts his stuff, beady black eyes sparkling, rattles his feathers and lofts his tail in that gorgeous rainbow spread – well, that's a show-stopper. Humans stand in awe.

In addition, both sexes have that adorable little row of stiff black feathers standing erect on their heads, looking for all the world like the old Roman helmets that gladiators wore. Even the tiny gray fuzzy chicks have that adornment, made all the more appealing by its diminutive size. "How great that you have peacocks," people say, and it is.

It's a good thing no one can see the peacock brain. It is what it is, generally adequate for the tasks peacocks are called on to perform, that is, basically nothing except scrounging for food and looking phenomenally good while doing it. Anything more complex taxes the pea-brain past endurance and sends the bird into a screaming frenzy. A peacock's panic voice is set about 50 decibels higher than the human ear can sustain for more than five minutes or so up close. It sounds eerily like a human cry for help and it takes only one scream to set off the whole flock. The sound reverberates through the countryside as birds from distant trees and bushes take up the cry. I'm sure there are neighbors who believe dire murder is being committed on a regular basis, but nobody has called the sheriff yet.

Anything can trigger mass hysteria on a grand scale; a stranger at the barn, a dog wandering into the wrong space, an approaching thunderstorm. Peacocks really hate thunderstorms, even worse than my big hairy cowards, but I guess if I slept in the top of a tree I'd hate lightning and hail even worse than I do.

We tend to forgive peacocks much because of their beauty. They dress up the place to such a high degree, we wash peacock poop off the sidewalk and say nothing. The incredible colors and intricate patterns of their tails when they strut through the sunlight excuses the sin of eating my garden plants left outside unprotected overnight. They raid the chicken feeders, scratch up the new grass, turn over the dog's water bucket and sound like Santa's reindeer on the roof, but we forget all that when we sit in the swing and watch them strutting and posturing in the yard.

First-year males look a lot like females in color and have no more tails than the hens. The males shed their tails in the summer and grow new ones in late winter, apparently with the sole purpose of impressing hens. You can estimate a peacock's age by the length and beauty of his tail. When they all begin to shed, the ground gleams with rainbow feathers everywhere. It always seems such a waste. The kids pick up great sheaves of them and stick them in jars and cans, play with the cats with them, tickle the dogs' bellies, tickle each other for that matter. Shorn of their glory, the males look pretty much like the females, except their long, graceful necks are a much more vivid blue.

Females, for the most part, are cool, but there seems to be a predisposition of males to become enamored of objects whose composition makes romance a remote if not downright impossible prospect. Observing them brings home the fact that they are not Mensa material.

One big handsome male carried on a torrid if one-sided courtship with an evaporative cooler for two or three summers. Every time we turned it on he appeared in a state of great excitement, posing and posturing as long as it was running. His love, as you may imagine, went unrequited, but he persisted until the cooler stopped running and was taken down. He may not have been too bright, but he was faithful.

Peacocks don't have a corner on quirky behavior, though. Guineas are perfectly enchanting birds, but even I would never claim that they are brainy. A lovely lavender guinea, still in her chickhood, fell hopelessly, devotedly in peacock love. She paired with a male when he was a mere tailless adolescent and was no less enamored of him then than she is today, when he sports a full-flowered rainbow appendage. Surprisingly, he seems to return her affection, for peacocks can be vicious to other poultry and yet the two are always together. I confess that I have been glad it seems to be platonic love, since I'm not sure chicks from such a union would have sense enough to exit the egg.

Still, their devotion is touching somehow. They are completely different, yet they share some common bond only they understand. There's a lesson in there somewhere.

Going With the Flow
Tops Control

Birds are absolutely fascinating creatures, from the caged and domesticated to the wild and natural. Quite aside from their innate physical beauty and their always-incredible ability to fly, they have unique personalities that provide endless amusement and sometimes-intense frustration for their human observers.

Birds are both prey and predator, depending on the species. A pair of large and gorgeous red-tailed hawks that live on our farm, swooping soundlessly low across the open pastures or soaring high above, seeking game, always raises the hair on my neck with their shrill calls and acrobatic flight. I'm grateful not to be a rabbit or a mouse in the grass below. The chickens flinch when the shadow of the hawk crosses them, though I've yet to see a hawk take one. Doesn't mean they haven't.

As hawks are predators, chickens are prey. Some of them just don't know it. I can pretty well imagine what goes on in a hawk's mind; fierce and straightforward, intent on survival, pragmatic and merciless in its quest for food for itself and nestlings. But what in the world is a chicken thinking when she spies the nice unturned patch of earth and flies across the fence to investigate it while four big, hairy dogs lie watching her as if she were a well-done steak? No hawk would pull such a dumb stunt.

In fact, I'm often driven to wonder what my chickens are thinking. I love my hens, but I would never defend their intelligence. They are creatures of habit, wooed by food and oblivious to danger until disaster rolls over them, at which time, in a cloud of feathers and a din of nerve-rending screams, they desperately try not to die.

The last batch of pullets I raised chose to roost on the cage I used to move them into the chicken yard. It sits by the gate even now. I tried moving it and caused such anxiety and confusion among the young hens that I put it back. Shortly after the move we had a fierce thunderstorm early in the evening. I looked out to check on the hens, certain they had retreated into the chicken house. There they all sat in the driving rain, hunkered down into their feathers, dripping wet and miserable.

I went out to save them. Grabbing them two at a time, I hauled them shrieking into the dark house and put them on the roost, causing a deafening gabble of protest from the older hens, all sensibly dry and presumably asleep. After numerous trips in the dark, cowering at the lightning flashes and the crashes of thunder, I didn't seem to be making much progress. There were as many dripping wet hens on the top of the cage as there had been to start with, except now they were standing, shaking out their feathers and complaining loudly. Every time I grabbed a couple they screamed as if they saw the chopping block, which caused everybody else to scream in panicky sympathy.

Finally I had sense enough to realize that I had carried the same two gray Brahmas with feathered legs into the house at least twice. I shook the water out of my face and saw the last two I'd stuffed onto the perch making a mad dash through the storm back to the cage.

The predator in me surfaced. I wished there was a chopping block in the yard. I tossed the two yelping hens in my hands onto the top of the cage and slogged back to the house, expecting at any moment to be rendered senseless by a lightning stroke and feeling it would serve me right for being as dumb as the chickens.

Shedding my soggy clothes and drying myself off, I reflected that those silly hens had free choice and could have gone into the chicken house not three feet away. They didn't feel safe there. For reasons known only to them, they felt better riding out the storm on top of their familiar cage.

I guess sometimes we just need to let things be instead of trying to control everything around us. The outcome may not be exactly what we planned, but maybe it doesn't have to be. In the case of the chickens, I at least would have stayed dry.

Go with the flow. You never know where it might take you.

On their way ...

Miss Kitty Is No More

Miss Kitty is no more. It grieves me mightily to say that; she has been the matriarch of the hen flock and my undisputed favorite for a long time. She was a big, fluffy Cochin, black and white striped, with abundant feathers on her legs and a knowing look in her eye. Her name derived from the fact that when I called the cats in the evening to come get their food, she beat them to the dish. Cat food was a great favorite of hers. She followed me about the yard when I was outside, never getting very far away. I'm sure she thought something yummy would appear at any moment and she didn't want to miss it.

None of the other hens messed with her; she was the biggest of them, but more than that, she had the confidence in herself that makes a leader. She even bossed the roosters and had two faithful suitors with whom she shared her favors when the notion took her. The kids could pick her up and carry her, and she looked for all the world like royalty being borne by choice to a destination she determined. Her bright brown eyes took in everything, and if I sat out in a chair in the evening, she sat companionably nearby on a small wooden table. We never said much, but it was a nice feeling, having her sitting there, thinking over the events of the day just past.

There wasn't a stupid thought in her head, unlike many hens I have known, and she laid a big, smooth, brown egg almost every day, in the third nest box, top row.

She was raised in the henhouse, just like all the rest of the flock, but as soon as they were released, she took to the giant elm tree in the chicken yard when it was time to roost. She would fly up to the lowest branch and march along it to a fork, which led her upward into the heart of the tree. From there she walked out onto a slender limb that bowed beneath her considerable weight, settled herself, and there she slept the night away. I could never get her into the chicken house for the night unless I was outside at the right time, picked her up before she ascended her tree and stashed her on the roost in the house.

Everything has a finite life span; I have learned this lesson well. All too soon our animal friends leave us behind. But Miss Kitty was only about three years old; I expected several more years of her companionship. However, the foxes have been visiting again. They don't come at night, when everything is locked up or roosting high in the trees. Their raids are made just after sunrise, when the grass is still wet and chilly and the day barely begun. The chickens have come down from their roost, but they are a bit sluggish still, not as quick and agile as they will be later, especially on a chilly morning. I have begun to find feathers here and there, attesting to the deadly struggle that took place while the rest of us slept, unaware.

The fox are bolder than they once were; the smaller of them has invaded the chicken yard, something they had not done before. The hen house is closed and locked at that hour, but there are the stubborn holdouts roosting in the giant elm just above it. Miss Kitty was one of those. I hope they killed her quickly, and that she didn't wish I would come to save her. I don't know whether chickens think like that, though I am totally convinced that dogs do. I am angry with the foxes; they never get roosters. It's not that I am ready to feed roosters to them, but how is it that only hens find their way down the russet scoundrels' throats?

The yard is emptier without Miss Kitty's presence, whether busily scratching for bugs under a bush or sitting serenely on the table next to my chair. The fox got two other hens before I found a way to hustle them all in every evening – a chore I didn't need. I regret them, but I don't miss their physical presence as I do hers. And somehow the nature of her death, natural though it may have been, is troubling to me. Violent death is hard to come to grips with; it comes not as a friend but as a screaming maniac shrouded with terror and shock and disbelief. There is so much of it loose in the world; I would spare anyone I could from that fearful specter.

Miss Kitty was only a hen, and not very important in the grand scheme of things. Certainly her loss is insignificant beside the losses of bright young people standing at the beginning of their world. They died for reasons that most of us simply cannot fathom, because no one listened to the warnings and took the steps that would have curbed a young man's rage and despair. The system, with its layers of legalities and checks and balances, failed. My mind and heart cannot bear the images and pain one man created for so many in one morning of utter madness, and so I turn away from it, helpless and hopeless in the face of such tragedy.

It is at least bearable to mourn the loss of my small friend, Miss Kitty.

A special little friend

71

It Takes a Village and Looks Like We're It

"It takes a village to raise a child" is a phrase familiar to most of us. I associate it with Hilary Clinton, but she didn't originate the idea, and I'm pretty sure she never lived in a village. Still, the meaning is clear; it takes a lot of effort and input from many different sources to raise a child. Humans don't always take advantage of the options they have when it comes to caring for their young; they tend to overlook resources like elder family members who have little to do with the time on their hands in favor of bright, noisy, busy daycare centers.

Of course, today's elders may be touring Alaska in their 2000 square foot RV, snorkeling off the coast of Florida, or training for the next Senior Marathon. Human children must make do with what they've got available.

Geese, on the other hand, rarely run marathons or volunteer at the library bake sale every weekend. They pretty much graze green grass, catch the odd grasshopper and clean up the fruit that fell from the trees in the orchard. Intersperse that with serious napping, a dip in the goose tanks a couple of times a day, grooming and preening and checking the feeders. By goose standards, it's a pretty full life.

In late winter and early spring there is a flurry of excitement in the flock. Sex rears its ugly head and the urge to procreate goes into overdrive. The air is rent with sounds of battle as the huge ganders challenge one another for their places in the pecking order, the higher the better. They entwine their long, slender necks and yank great mouthfuls of feathers out of one another while shrieking the vilest insults a birdbrain could possibly formulate. Their great wings batter at one another as they circle, each watching for an opportunity to gain a good hold on the other. The geese wait nearby, watching the fray intently, now and then making short little runs along the ground, flapping their wings as if this time they might lift off into the air and be gone forever.

They never do. Once the ganders have settled between them who is Boss and who is lower down on the totem pole, the geese breed with them in the water tanks, flapping and squawking in dubious ecstasy amid showers of silver drops beaten up from the water's surface by their powerful wings. And once bred, they begin to lay.

Good night Nellie, do they ever lay! Great smooth white eggs with shells so hard you don't see how a gosling could ever break through it. The huge nests on the ground are filled with eggs, sometimes thirty or more unless they are stolen; the gooses' skirts will not spread wide enough to cover them all. Sometimes we remove a few, just so the rest will have a better chance at hatching, but it's an adventure. A goose is just like a game chicken when it comes to her eggs, only a lot bigger. She doesn't just sit there observing and wish you well in your endeavors. Her long, graceful neck stretches to double its normal length, she opens her mouth and emits a chilling hiss which lets you know in no uncertain terms that she means business and she wants you gone. Should you be foolhardy enough to ignore her, having believed someone who told you she was bluffing and wouldn't hurt you, you will quickly find that statement to be untrue. She will hurt you. She will grab hold of you with her substantial beak and bite down hard enough to make you squeal, and then she will add insult to injury by twisting the mouthful of you in her beak sharply enough to make you roar. Bloodletting is possible here.

Meanwhile, every other goose and gander on the place is circling you and their peer like Sitting Bull around Custer, shrieking insults and threats and even attempting a few nips of their own on unguarded spots of your anatomy. It seems the better part of valor just to leave the nests alone and let whatever eggs will hatch do their thing. Following this line of thinking helps to keep the goose population under control, since not many eggs ever hatch. Still, every year a few do, and this year is no exception.

That's where the village thing comes into play. Unless you see the goose get off the nest, it's next to impossible to determine which large white bird is the mommy and which are the aunties. They are all strutting and preening, necks outstretched and heads craned around to observe the little ones, just out of the egg, trying to figure out the vast world they have tumbled into. Sometimes, if you're lucky, the babies that hatch first stay in the nest with Mama until she's ready to leave the eggs. Then you can stash the little family, entire, in a cage until the youngsters are too big for fox bait.

We weren't that lucky today. On a very stressful day, with already more to do than would ever get done, a commotion amongst the flock led Papa to the discovery of three downy chartreuse goslings with bright orange legs and smoky little heads. They were the focus of attention for about eight big white geese as well as for the African flock, both loudly claiming them. The poor babies, tolled from the nest where their mother still sat on eggs, didn't know where they belonged, or to whom, and probably didn't care. They just needed a warm place under somebody to rest awhile, and there were no volunteers.

The African flock numbers nine or so great gray geese with knobs on their beaks at the forehead. They are noisy, aggressive, and will have nothing to do with the white flock, which numbers about eight.

75

There are some white ones with gray flecks among their feathers, crossbreds, but they are relegated to the white flock as well. Never the twain shall congregate at the water tanks together; it is Africans first and white whenever Africans get tired of hogging the water. It is a white goose who still sits on the nest, but made no attempt to keep the goslings from leaving and following the other geese away from the warmth and safety of her nest.

Papa put the babies in a big cage along with two of the most maternal appearing geese, and hoped for the best. About midnight, dead tired, we remembered the goslings and went to check on them. Several white geese were circling the cage, talking quietly among themselves. The two inside were keeping pace with them while the babies huddled together miserably on the ground, chilled and ignored.

The spare bathroom now sports a giant box with a heat lamp attached to it, sharing space with the cage containing three baby peacocks. In the box three poufy little goslings preen and chatter softly under the warmth of the light. We have become the village required to raise these particular babies. Sara is enchanted.

Reason enough to give them house room.

Chapter 4

Seasons Drive the Weather and the Weather Drives Our Lives

Memories of Spring Provide Entertainment for a Long Hot Summer

Spring moves on the balls of its feet, light as the fluff from a milkweed plant bouncing on the breeze. As soon as the sun appears in the morning, before its rays have a chance to warm the birds waking from the chilly night, spring begins its merry chase of the daylight hours. There is haste in every hour, every minute; life is full out, breakneck speed, no hesitation. The air itself is electric, stirring with eagerness, charged with life.

Sometimes it seems you can hear the grass growing after a good rain. The earth goes from brown to green overnight and the evening's grass is half again as tall as it was just that morning. Plants pierce the soil with sharp pointed slivers of tender green that toughen within hours to present a set of leaves tight on a lengthening stem and before you know it, flowers open to the sun. There is nothing slow or shy about the blankets of bluebonnets, the windrows of cowslips, the delicate bruises of winecups, the spiky stems of Indian paintbrush, the lemony blobs of buttercups dotting the ditches and filling the fields.

Hedges of honeysuckle, muted green all winter, suddenly spark to life, sending out pale green tendrils loaded with tightly closed buds that one day burst into long, unbelievably delicate blossoms. They intoxicate the world with an unmistakable scent more definitive than the most expensive man-made perfume. That fragrance is familiar to anyone who grew up in the South, and brings back memories of childhood: caves under the swinging vines, sucking the sweet nectar out of the flowers one by one, the steady hum of honeybees round your head, cool moist earth under your bare feet, secrets you promised never to tell a living soul whispered in your ears, and all of it wrapped in that deliciously heady mantle of honeysuckle.

Gardens begin to take shape, changing overnight, it seems, from the sturdy, small plants set so painstakingly into the open ground to thriving thickets of cilantro, tomatoes, peppers, onions, reaching for sunlight, for water, for food from the earth. Squash plants boom out of the ground, doubling in size in a few days, great serrated leaves arching upward on big hollow stems, bright golden blossoms glowing beneath them.

Weeds proliferate, uninvited relatives, upstarts that outgrow the beans and cucumbers; tough cousins from the wrong side of the tracks that grab all the good stuff for themselves and shade out the more genteel residents until they are pulled or chopped or otherwise disposed of. They go to seed early, practiced survivors, wily in the art of reproducing themselves as soon as possible; tilling the rows only brings forth a new horde of them to be dealt with. Rain makes them impossible and drought doesn't faze them; only violence does them in.

The wind is restless in the trees, sometimes all through the night. It races across the sky, often far too high for us to feel, bringing currents of cold air and rivers of tropical moisture together so that they collide high above us and blind us with lightening, deafen us with thunder, drench us with rain, pound us with hail. The morning after such a storm the sky is placid as a summer lake, blue as a baby's eyes, but the springtime frenzy is up there, starting all over again. Stepping outside, you can feel it flowing as a torrent of snowmelt dashes down slope to the sea, great currents of air clashing with one another, poised for another round.

Babies are ready to be born. They have lain in their mother's bellies all winter, growing; spring calls them forth on their own schedules, which have nothing to do with us. The great placid cows move slowly, their knowledge of what lies ahead weighting them down as their time approaches. When all is complete and the time is right, they seek out a private spot, away from the herd, and lie down. If all goes well the new life begins; wobbly legs, big soft eyes, hungry mouth seeking milk that the mother has ready. In no time the calf is following behind her, stronger with every nursing, and in just a few days is racing across the evening field with others just like him, tail straight up and young heart pounding as he celebrates his life with all its joy throbbing through him.

Lambs and kids are born much the same way, quicker on their feet, maybe, full of wonder at the world they have fallen into and making the most of every moment. Chicks hatch and peep at their mother's skirts, rushing to her urgent announcement of some delectable bug or grub scratched up out of the ground for them, settling beneath her for a nap, small heads poking out here and there from her maternal mound. She glows fierce and prideful, full of life pulsing beneath her, her own life fulfilled and her patience rewarded.

Everything grows and thrives and pushes at every boundary it encounters. There's no time to waste, things are happening, life will not be put off for a second. If you must run to keep up, why then you had better run; nothing will wait. Even nights are filled with restless tossings and turnings, waiting for morning so it all can begin again.

Spring will lengthen and fade. Summer will come hard on its heels and with it long, slow days of sun glare and dry heat; drowsy afternoons that stretch into long evenings and hot, star-filled nights. The undercurrent of urgency will drain away and a quieter rhythm takes its place. It will be time to grow and mature and enter the next phase of the journey. It will come none too soon for many of us, exhausted by the unrelenting pace of spring.

And what fine memories we'll have to entertain us on long summer evenings under the stars.

Splendor!

Summer Wears Flowers and Ladybugs

Summer puts a taste on the tongue, a feel on the skin, a mellow flush all over that leads to lassitude. Fall sharpens the senses, invigorates the mind; winter wraps the body in layers of protection against the raw wind and wet skies, and there is a darkening of the heart that can happen sometimes; spring brings an awakening of all things that grow and change. But summer, though a season in the natural progression, is apart from all the others.

Summer wears flowers in its hair and ladybugs in its clothes. It hums and buzzes and drowses through long afternoons of heat that shimmer the ripening hay fields and turn tomatoes red as blood among their dark green leaves. The rich air is heavy with heady draughts of honeysuckle, weighted with scents from a hundred plants one never sees, thick with humidity that makes a body slow its pace, like it or not. Sweet though it can be, summer in Texas is not for the faint of heart.

Morning comes hazy, sunlight muted through rising mist from the valley. Standing outside with a cup of coffee, looking down the valley where the vapor is coming off the creek, I know it's as cool as it will be all day. Wherever the sun strikes, its heat portends the day to follow, and whatever work can be done early, so much the better. It's the best garden time, before the day sucks the juice right out of both plants and gardener. Barn chores are easier before the barns get hot and airless. Always the smart ones, animals go out to graze and they work at it earnestly, filling up after the night's sleep. The sun climbs quickly, haze burned away, the day beginning to simmer.

Afternoons are long, not measured in hours but in increments of heat. By mid-afternoon the cattle are all lying down somewhere under the trees. Somehow they know where the best place to catch a breeze will be that given day and they gather there, calves lying together and cows spaced around them, cudding comfortably through the hottest hours. The horses stand drowsing, one hind foot cocked, tails swishing, making a pass now and again at an irritating fly. Although their eyes are almost closed and they appear to rest, their ears are alive, always listening to a world they never fully trust to be benign. Sweat is dried on their backs.

If you're out and about, there isn't much to see. Small things are hunkered down, waiting for the heat to pass. Sometimes a snake will be stretched out basking in the sun; so lethargic from the heat it will scarcely notice you until you're right up close. If you press it, the long, sleek body will move silently into the nearest cover and disappear, a haughty glance lingering behind. Once in awhile you will jump a rabbit, especially if you have a dog along, and it will leap away, veering right and left as if demented, and coming to rest not so far away from where you startled it, eyes wide and frantic, ears standing straight up.

In midsummer, the dog will probably look at the rabbit and then at you, tongue lolling, plainly saying it just isn't worth the effort.

People are out, of course. Tractors are weaving their regular patterns across the hay fields, leaving great swaths of hay lying in windrows behind the cutters. Some tractors have air-conditioned cabs now, with radios to pass the long hot hours alone. Many do not, sporting only a canopy to keep off the worst of the sun. Papa's tractor is one of those; he wears a big hat and carries a thermos of water. He also sees and hears things he never would in one of the air-conditioned cabs. It's a tradeoff.

When Papa was plowing up his oats to plant haygrazer, he became aware that a big female red-tailed hawk was watching him. She sat on an upturned clod at the edge of the field just where he made his turn and kept her yellow eyes fixed on him, turning slowly on the clod as he passed and watching as he made the journey up the field and back down to where she sat. He made about ten rounds like that, thinking she might be watching for field mice in the freshly turned earth, but she never made a move to hunt. She just sat watching him.

Suddenly, as he made his approach, she leaped from the clod, great wings beating the heavy air, and was aloft. She circled him a few times and then was gone. He said it was as if she was curious about what he was doing, and when she had satisfied her curiosity, she went on about her business.

She was one of the perks of the open-air tractor.

After the long, hot day evening finally comes and things perk up. Cattle get up and begin to graze; the horses come up for feed and to get a drink. Even the goats go out into the front pasture for an hour's munching. Sitting in the swing, looking down the valley, everything feels just right. Another hot day behind us, perhaps a little breeze or the rumbling promise of a shower refreshing us, we watch the evening come down. The trio of tiny screech owls lines up on the fence to wait their turn at the birdbath where they drink, their little button eyes gleaming in the dusk. The honeysuckle down on the fence sends waves of sweetness across the pasture right into our faces as we settle tired bodies toward the night.

Sometimes, even in Texas in the summer, you just want to live forever.

Fall Festivals are Fine, But What Happened To Plain Old Halloween

Finally, October weather! The only thing is, now it's November. Oh, well, we'll take fine days any way we can get them. That snap to in the air in the evening is invigorating, no matter when it comes. It's nice to hunt up a jacket and put on jeans, though Papa disdains such behavior, luxuriating in his short shirtsleeves and poking fun at those of us who want a little more. I will admit, I've seen some folks recently bundled up in parkas and gloves and I have to wonder what they plan to add when/if it gets really cold. Amarillo has already gotten into the 30's and had snow, leading to a certain amount of nostalgia on my part.

The trees of Central Texas are nice, but once you live in the big sky country, it always has a claim on your heart. Up there, you wear a big jacket when the north wind blows; it can cut right through you. When a blue norther sweeps in you can see it coming, a low, smooth roll of clouds arching from horizon to horizon, moving like a freight train. One moment it's bright and warm and the next the north wind slaps you in the face and takes your breath. Sometimes there are no clouds, but the line in the sky is there all the same, marking the front pushing down from the north. The old saying is that in the Panhandle, there's nothing between the North Pole and you but a barbed wire fence, and somebody left the gap down.

We don't have that here. Fronts may come in cold, but they've been moderated by grassland and low rolling country. There's no frigid breath from the winter giant whistling down the back of your neck and up your sleeves, making your ears hurt and your lungs ache and your eyes burn. It's much more gradual; a damper chill that builds in intensity until you suddenly realize you're cold. Most usually there's time to get ready in all the ways you need to. Pipes get wrapped, plants get covered, animals get extra feed and shelter. In Amarillo, the change is more extreme; more than once we had roses in the snow.

Mother Nature must love that part of Texas. She sure pulls out all the stops to put on a show, no matter the season. From lightning storms to snow to just plain perfect days, she gives it her all.

Old Mom Nature is no slouch around here, of course. She keeps us hopping, sometimes literally. Papa came in the other day from feeding cows and I noticed he was barefoot and muddy almost to the knees.

"What shall I do with these?" he asked, waving a pair of once-white socks in my general direction. Seems he was in the lot with the cows, pulling the string covering off a new round bale of hay when the mud grabbed hold and sucked his boot off. In the struggle to stay upright, hang on to the hay string, and feel around trying to get his foot back in the boot, he lost his balance and the other boot came off.

He gave me the socks and departed for the shower. It was Grandson Two's birthday and we were late for the festivities. It's just been a wealth of festivities around here, like it is every year. Grandson One was born the day before Halloween and Grandson Two the day after, so we've always had a 3-day celebration, more or less.

Halloween was great; the weather was perfect. There seemed to be fewer houses decorated and lit than last year, but there were still a bunch. You would have to be small of heart not to get a bang out of all the little spooks charging up to your door, eyes sparkling, to beg candy. I'm not sure where the tradition started, but I hope it doesn't die out completely. "Fall Festivals" are fine, but plain old Halloween is terrific fun. Little people don't associate it with dark powers and evil intentions; all that mumbo-jumbo is for adults who have nothing better to focus on. Children see it as a deliciously scary, hilarious romp with friends scooping up candy. At least, the children I know feel that way. Let them have their happily spooky night, uncomplicated by grownup baggage.

There were lots of kids having a good time on Halloween night, and the grandparents weren't doing too badly, either. A little walking, a lot of laughing and a little smizzle of chocolate once in awhile make for a very happy evening. Then there were the birthdays; remembrances of happy days when children were born, a lot of laughing, a few tears for years fled so fast, and a little more chocolate. Do you see a pattern here?

On to Thanksgiving!

"Neither Rain Nor Snow Nor Dark Of Night..."

Well, hello, El Niño! We've been patiently – more or less – waiting for his influence to kick in and give us some much-needed moisture. I guess we were a little strong in our wishing for it, because the eventuality exceeded the expectations. While we were told that it wasn't that bad in town, it was a bit dicey out in the western reaches of the county. Nowhere near as bad as it was about ten years ago, when we lost power for over five days running and I was cooking for two little boys on a Coleman camp stove and trying to explain why there was no PBS, but cold and icy just the same. Since the fireplace is our main source of heat in the house, we have burned a lot of wood these last few days.

The kids have enjoyed it. Kids enjoy a lot of things that are stressful for adults, precisely because they are kids and have no clue how difficult things can get if the power goes out or the water freezes solid. They knocked icicles down and slid on the slick patches and danced in the snow flurries with their tongues out to taste the flakes. After an intense but fruitless search for her boots, Sara ended up skidding over here anyhow to have a hot biscuit and play a few fast games of Blink! with Papa. The ground was frozen, so the lack of boots didn't matter, but in the aftermath, we'd better find the boots.

It's always distressing when there is a cold, steady rain that wets the cattle to the skin, followed by wind and temperatures below freezing for hours and hours. They stand at the hay bale and eat without pausing; between meals they back up against a barn with tails tucked and heads down, the picture of misery, enduring. There is no dry place to lie down, but some do, especially the calves. Feed is essential, and hay disappears like the ice will when the sun finally shows itself. Nights are particularly hard; the cold grips harder in the long, dark hours before sunrise.

Even with Papa's good preparations, somewhere water freezes and breaks a pipe or faucet. Stock tanks freeze over and the ice must be broken so the cows can drink. Papa ties the floats up on a couple of them and the overflow keeps the water open, making a fanciful plume of ice cascade down the side of the tank. Near the bottom, the huge goldfish stir sluggishly, all but dormant in the frigid water. Someday we're getting a couple of heated automatic waterers for the big stock, but not as long as hay costs $85 and up for one bale, if and when you can find it.

Papa is planning to get his meteorological license, or whatever you have to have to predict weather, asap. He has said all along that as soon as we had frost and all the pastures went dormant it would start raining. He has a new prediction – it will still be raining when it's time to plant spring crops but will quit as soon as the seeds are in the ground. On the positive side – and there always is one - we have now had the required hours below 40 degrees required for a peach crop and the moisture should help the trees this year. Last year was the first season in over 35 years that we had a total crop failure in the orchard. With as many trees as we have, that in itself is a major disaster. Sara and Papa were not able to pick and eat a single fresh peach.

There are extra blankets down for the big hairy cowards, all of whom are inside except for brief potty breaks. I would like to relieve what I perceive as their boredom by giving them big chew bones, but the resulting mayhem wouldn't be worth it. They would amuse themselves by standing stiff-legged over a chosen bone and threatening dismemberment and death to anyone approaching it, which would instantly render it the only desirable bone in the place, whereupon they would all fall upon one another with mad abandon. I'm not up to that kind of fracas in this weather.

Mostly because my hands are screaming and my nose is numb from taking buckets of hot water out to melt the frozen waterers in the chicken house, gathering up cat feeding pans and renewing the crates and boxes I have fixed for them to sleep in. I can't be certain, but I think they must play musical beds at night, because a neatly stacked and arrayed selection of blanketed crates at bedtime is a total shambles by daylight.

The pushface pack seldom strays far from the radiator heaters or the bed in front of the fireplace. The sound of food being dished up in the kitchen pulls them out of the blankets, and after a trip outdoors they often engage in a tussle, but for the most part they stay tucked in. It's nice, hearing the crackle of the fire punctuated by gentle bulldog snores from under blankets around the room. Tess, the Frenchie, is on official squirrel patrol since the bird feeders are busy, so she bombs out the door like a short black kamikaze, scattering squirrels and birds alike. She takes her role very seriously, and cold is no deterrent.

It has deterred just about everybody else, though. Much to my surprise, the mail didn't run during this little fracas with Mother Nature, and we have an outstanding mailman. My earliest memories are involved with the Postal service, my brother being third generation in its employ. That old oath about "neither rain nor snow nor dark of night shall stay this postman from his appointed rounds" – well, something like that – apparently no longer applies. Admittedly, our mail is hardly exciting, as a rule, but still … I wonder if they've heard about this in Minnesota? I hear it snows a lot up there.

Snow in Central Texas is rare and a joy for all to behold for the short time it lasts.

What's a Little Mud

Feast or famine, that seems to be nature's take on things. We went from blasted, parched, cracked-open ground to torrents of water cascading across the yard in virtual rivers, washing leaves and twigs and small branches into deep curving eddies and ultimately rushing down the driveway. Water ran out of the soaked fields and filled the bar ditches, which delivered the flow into the small creeks and tributaries, swelling Berry's Creek into a rolling brown out-of-banks torrent headed, I guess, for the lake.

Harry Potter detractors, take note: there is nothing less than magic involved in rain like this in Texas in August. The whole dusty, bedraggled landscape takes on a new look, a scrubbed fresh face. Pastures seared yellow and crackly underfoot by the relentless summer sun overnight sprout sprigs of bright green life. Now that's magic! The horses and cattle have left the hay bale and are once again grazing, nipping off the delicate, tender growth eagerly.

Rain brightens the whole world out here. Drooping grapevines, dropping shoals of dry yellow leaves onto the wilted grass, perk up at once. Bois d' arc trees, along with the fruit trees, suffer terribly in dry heat. Their leaves grow dull and limp, looking as if one good gust of wind would send them spiraling down. Good rains plump the leaves right back up and seem to lift the branches in thanks for the drink.

The chickens were heedless of the rain, walking around with draggly feathers dripping, scrutinizing the ground for bugs and worms just like always. Rain helps them out by making the ground softer for scratching. The ducks were really happy. During the downpours they were dabbling and dibbling, paddling and flapping in the pond their pen became, loudly declaring their delight. And yes, "quack" is exactly the sound they make.

As with everything in life there is of course a downside. Delightful as the rain is on many levels, rain equals mud. In a household like ours, that means mud everywhere, outside and in. Four paws times four bulldogs equals sixteen muddy paws coming and going. It might not be so bad if all four weren't overcome with ecstasy at being reunited with me after fifteen minutes out in the yard, but they are. Every single time. I always find it irresistible, those bright brown eyes and ear-to-ear bulldog grins, but I could do without the muddy streaks on my legs and the carpet of paw prints on the tile floor resulting from their tango of joy.

Yes, I do keep a large towel by the door to wipe their paws with, but there are sixteen paws, all muddy and all scrambling to be the first up on me.

They should be trained to enter sedately and sit quietly waiting their turn, but bulldogs are seldom sedate and anyhow, even my grandkids don't do that. The bulldogs, having just left bold muddy streaks on the sliding glass door as far up as they can reach, are pushing and shoving each other to be first to burst through the door. I might make a swipe at a paw as it flies past, but it's really just a token gesture. They are moving too fast.

Add to the mix Obi, a Pug who believes he is a Rottwieler, and things get really interesting, since Riggs the Heeler lives in the back yard. Riggs is good-tempered but will accept insults only up to a point, and Obi passed that point some time ago. They coexist in the yard just fine, but there's something about Obi's coming into the house that triggers an all-out, take no prisoners battle about half the time. Obi clearly will be the loser here if the fray is allowed to run its course, as he is outweighed by 30 pounds and outgunned on every count, but he remains convinced he can take Riggs, prior evidence to the contrary notwithstanding.

So I speak loudly and carry a fearsome flyswatter to change Obi's mind about doing battle. Riggs always stops at a word from me unless the conflict is deeply joined, i.e. he has Obi by the back of the neck, pinning him to the concrete. Even then he leaves off and stalks away, giving me a reproachful look as if to say, "What do you expect me to do when the little twerp calls me that?" I grab Obi, still yelping canine obscenities, and drag him into the house. At least I can wipe his feet. Meanwhile the other three whirling dervishes have slung mud far and wide. I sometimes feel like a cleaning machine, sprouting brooms and mops and suction devices in a vain attempt to keep up with the mayhem.

Oh, well. I love rain after drought and bulldogs all the time. What's a little mud between friends?

Did you feel something on your foot?

Rules, Rules, Rules

August comes to its end not a moment too soon for me. It's never been my favorite month and this one especially has been a killer. Triple digit heat and barren, blazing skies for days on end is not my idea of a way to live. Add to that the pressures of school beginning again, and it's hard to find much to like about August. Heat turns minor irritations into major malfunctions, and major malfunctions become very big deals indeed. I don't think straight with sweat dripping into my eyes and my brain fried by the sun. My main goal is to get somewhere cool and stay there. While filling the myriad water buckets and bowls and fountains around here, trying to keep geese and chickens and dogs hydrated, I focus on January. Checking on floats that keep water tanks filled and watering plants that wilt daily in the furnace blast of afternoon, I try to recreate the way north wind feels on my face when a cold front blows in.

My granma used to say, "Don't wish time away," and I almost never do, until August. Of course, there are redemptions for the miserable month. The little screech owls have been active lately, calling back and forth from trees around the house when they visit the birdbaths for an evening drink. Mourning doves return, their plaintive calls full of some old melancholy no one really understands. Perhaps they know dove season is on the horizon, though why anyone would hunt them mystifies me. Some early mornings border on fresh, the stirring of air almost cool. And there is nothing more wonderful or welcome than rain on a hot August day. First a darkening of the sky, low thunder mutterings, anticipation, and then the smell of warm rain on hot earth. Old memories of summers past mingle with gratitude for the respite from heat.

Best of all, I guess, the moon rises late and lush, its color deepening as it waxes to a full orange orb riding low on the eastern horizon. It looks like a butterscotch candy, growing fat and full until it begins to wane, one side paring down as candy does when you lick it. The winter moon is white and cold, but an August moon bathes the pastures in rich golden light while it lasts. I hate to go inside sometimes, lost in looking at it, knowing I won't see that particular moon ever again.

And after all, if we didn't live through August, we'd never get to October. August fosters patience and endurance. It seems we can learn something from every experience we have. For some of us the learning is easy, happening almost without our noticing until we look up and say, "Of course!." Others of us have a harder time, anticipating and trying to second-guess things until we're in such a state we can't see what it is we need to know until much later.

Grandson One moves through the world as confident and poised as a dancer. If he has doubts and anxieties, he keeps them to himself. His motto seems to be, "I can handle it". So it was with school beginning this year. It was time for him to be in school rather than at home and he wasted no time lamenting it; why worry over things that you cannot change? It is what it is. In this he mirrors both Papa and his parents, and it stands him in good stead. His standard reply for the inane question, "how was school?" has always been "good". Whatever happened or didn't happen is past and he feels little need to rehash it all, with some rare exceptions.

Grandson Two is the "feely" one. Things go harder for him, always. Every word, every gesture, every nuance weighs on him; did he do the right thing or the wrong thing? Was he rude (never) or thoughtless (hardly) and should he have done/said/been different? A people pleaser to the hilt, he was worried about meeting new teachers (would they like him?) and how the day would go. He rides a shuttle bus after school and he worried about getting on the right bus. His mother assured him that he had a bus card and she had written the appropriate notes; all would be well. But what, he asked, if they make me get on the wrong bus? Nonsense, she said, they won't do that.

Guess what? They did. He had quite a ride, along with some other kids, before he finally got to his destination. In this case, the lesson was clear and plain; the worse thing he could think of happened and he did just fine. Now if he can just master cursive writing, he will be okay.

As for Sara, the kindergarten girl, after two days she was tired from the long hours. She comes every day after school almost as if she wants to be sure things haven't changed. How is school for her? "Good. But rules, rules, rules! Too many rules! You can't even go down the slides on your tummy!"

In the grand scheme of things, shouldn't you be able to go down the slides on your tummy if you want to?

Sauce for the Goose...

Where was I? How did I miss winter entirely? Oh, wait, it's only the beginning of January. It just feels like spring, and not a very pleasant spring, at that. More the kind of spring you would just as soon skip, going straight to summer just to get it over with so that maybe cooler, more pleasant weather would follow. How did we get from the wettest season on record to the driest? Feast or famine seems to be the rule here.

Any time black dirt turns into powdery dust that puffs up under your feet when you walk, that's dry. The lawn croaked long ago, but even when conditions are bad, there are some patches of grass left that hold the promise of green if they can just get a little water. Not so now. It's all just dead. The pasture is crunchy underfoot, so dry that it feels as if the very thought of fire would set it off. Ours is too short to burn much, but the trees and underbrush are nothing but tinder right now.

The very air is dry, almost unheard of in this part of the world. It must be like this in the desert; hot in the daytime and chilly at night. Low humidity is great in many ways, but I hate to see the grandkids' mouths chapped and sore; why do little people lick their lips constantly once they get a little dry? I bought lip balm and greased them up, right down

Sara's alley since she thinks lipstick is way cool. Also way cool is the spark of static electricity that jumps from one person to another with just a bit of friction from shuffling across the carpet. West Texas residents are familiar with that spark, being accustomed to the tingle of grabbing a doorknob too fast when exiting a room, but the grandkids are not, and they love the tiny crackle on contact.

It's a bit uncomfortable, waiting to see what turn things will take. Will it rain in time to get hay planted, and then rain enough to make a cutting, or will this be one of those years when there is no local hay and anything you can find is incredibly expensive? "Experts" are talking about how the weather pattern is the same as the one in the '30's, when the Dust Bowl happened. If they can't make us nuts enough with the bird flu thing, maybe they can do it with the weather.

Rain would be nice. Beautiful sunsets feed the soul, but hay feeds cows and horses. Dry, sunny days are great for hiking and the spandex crowd's biking, but green grass makes horses slick off and get fat after the winter, and that takes rain. After so many days of dry wind and open sky, long, cool, gray days of slow rain and nights waking to the sound of low thunder and water dripping from the eaves sounds like heaven. Even muddy dog tracks everywhere doesn't sound so bad, at least not right now.

If only we could work out a trade with California; some of their wet weather for some of our sunshine.

If I am confused by the turn of events, weather-wise, I am not alone. Some of the feathered residents of the farm seem a bit addled as well. Or maybe the situation is just coming to light coincidentally. Remember the peacock/guinea pair, so firmly and fondly bonded for years? Well, now there's trouble in Paradise, at least from the guinea point of view.

I raised sixteen guinea keets last summer and had them penned, loath to release them to fend for themselves. The fox has not been in evidence lately, but guineas who fly into dog yards have a life expectancy of roughly thirty seconds, and since they are absolute pea-brains I figure about half of them will manage to do just that. However, they had long since outgrown the pen, and Papa released them.

Oh, joy unbounded! They leaped and capered and half-flew and crackled and cackled and chased one another until the dirt was thoroughly stirred up. The geese watched with their usual dignified hauteur, several roosters got into the mix but quickly exited, and several young peacocks came to play. Along came the peacock/guinea pair, drawn by the noise. The guinea was pretty excited by seeing sixteen birds just like her all in a merry group; she had seen them everyday in the pen, but apparently they look different outside of it, for she had never given them a moment's attention before. She soon tired of them, however, and turned to her companion...

...who was amazed, delighted, overwhelmed at the gorgeous array of guinea fowl capering before him. He looked like I think a Kansas farm boy might look upon stepping foot on the campus at Berkeley; he just couldn't believe his eyes. Forgotten was the peacock's longtime partner, his faithful little follower, his guinea fowl mate. His tail was fanned and he was telling the new group of lovelies what a fine figure he cut around the barnyard. They had accomplished what all the handsome peahens had been unable to do; lure him away from his little guinea girlfriend. She followed along forlornly, no match for the new girls on the block. As for me, I was terribly disappointed in the failure of true love.

Sunset ended the encounter, since all concerned found convenient trees to roost in for the night. I didn't see whether the pair went to roost together as is their wont, but I hope when morning comes she is pecking up breakfast with one of the handsome guinea guys.

Sauce for the goose, or something like that.

Chapter 5

The Light at the End of the Tunnel Is Grandkids

You're Just Not A Very Good Looker

Rating the twelve months, on a scale of one to twelve, August comes in at about twenty-two for me. Its only redeeming feature is being the last hurrah of summer, which can't draw to a close too fast. While this hasn't been such a bad summer for triple-digits, it still hasn't been that great.

Grandsons are back in school, having moved up a grade. They are in different schools, but they love the schools they're in and the teachers they have. Open houses were good experiences for both of them, and we all had a good feeling afterward, so when Grandson One walked in on the afternoon of the first day, I was interested in his reaction.

"So", I asked as the requisite snack was being prepared, "how was it?" Leaning against the cabinet and regarding me solemnly, he answered, "Good".

"All right, that makes 9,872 'goods' from you when I asked how your day at school was," I said. "How was it really?"

"Good," he said. "It was good. But I'll tell you, that teacher talked just a little too much. All day, talk, talk, talk."

Being a man of few words, I could see how this might bother him. On the other hand, I pointed out, on the first day of school there might have been a lot of things he needed to be told.

"I guess," he said doubtfully. "We'll see how she does tomorrow."

I am happy to report that her performance on the next day measured up to his expectations and he is very happy with her. Now all we have to worry about is whether the feeling is mutual.

The other Grandson was ecstatic for the first couple of days and then inquired of his mother when she thought the fun would start. We have no idea what he meant by that, since he seems to like his class and teacher a lot. Perhaps he had something specific in mind that happens when you get older, and it didn't materialize. At least not yet.

Sara will be in preschool again, and doesn't start until after Labor Day. For now it's a pleasure to have her all day; it's like sunrise several times a day. She makes things seem much less stressful and puts things in perspective with a few innocent words.

The other morning I was having no luck finding things I needed and frustration had set in. After several failed attempts to locate keys and my telephone book, I said in exasperation, "I have turned this place upside down and I can't find anything this morning!"

Sara was sitting in the floor with a couple of dogs, eating goldfish crackers. She looked up at me seriously for a moment and then shook her head, returning to her munching.

"Well, Gigi," she said, "I guess you're just not a very good looker."

After I got through laughing, all the stuff that was lost turned up. I sure am going to miss her when she starts school.

Sometimes Leaving Home Is Painful

There are grandparents who see their grandchildren twice a year and feel that is quite sufficient. Other grandparents see their grandchildren only a few times a year and suffer pangs of longing to be able to see them more often. It might depend partly on the grandchildren. The luckiest ones, in our opinion, see the kids almost every day. Papa and I are among that fortunate group.

It can be a mixed blessing. There are days when, perhaps, everything hurts and all that sounds good is a nice lie-down with a book, a couple of ibuprofen and a cup of something hot, with a bulldog draped over my legs snoring gently. Sara and the boys are somewhat sympathetic to that, but there are always lots of things to do, so mostly I get up when they come in. Truth is, I usually feel better; it's probably the company I keep.

There are also days when responsibilities weigh heavier than on other days, and things need tending to. Those are the days when Sara wants to paint, or one of the boys has a project he needs help with, or everybody sort of disappears and the sudden quiet makes me too nervous to focus on what I'm doing until I find out what they're doing. Every parent/grandparent knows that too noisy beats too quiet by a mile; they aren't usually doing anything too illegal if you can hear them doing it. It's the quiet stuff that means trouble. Painting a dog red, for example, is a fairly quiet activity except for the giggles of delight and the dog's tail knocking over paint cans, but the results are far-reaching and can be disastrous, so it's generally better to nip that kind of thing in the bud.

Sometimes having the kids around all day is just not long enough and thoughts of them keep popping up after they go home. Other days, half an hour is a lifetime and the echoing quiet left in their wake is a marvelous blessing. It all depends on where I am and where they are and how the signs read and whether we're having a weather front and if the moon is full. Other conditions may apply. I don't analyze it because there usually isn't time.

I do know that whatever the circumstance and despite how it all turns out, life comes into the house when the door bangs open and somebody shouts "Gigi!". I can't imagine living without that. Happily, the kids apparently agree.

Papa and I made arrangements to meet some old and dear friends from California at a designated spot in North Texas for a couple of days of chin-wagging while they were in Texas recently. I began making lists and lists of lists for the array of people who would take over the care of my big hairy cowards and my small, spoiled bulldogs and the incredible assortment of everything else I daily attend to. The grandkids reacted predictably. Grandson One, the pragmatic, hands-off one, allowed as how he hoped we had a good time, he would see us when we got back (if, I suspect, it falls into his busy schedule), and we're good to go. Grandson Two asked several anxious questions, promised to take care of the salt water aquarium and help with the birds, and wanted to be sure we would tell him goodbye before we left.

Sara almost convinced me not to go. She called on the phone after she went home at night, crying. Why did we have to go, she asked. Why were we leaving her behind, she wailed. Why, oh why, didn't we just stay home, a request punctuated by such heart rending sobs that I was ready to say okay, we don't need to go, it's only been six years or so since I left the place and I don't like to travel anyhow. It was suggested (rather heartlessly, I thought) that Sara was working it and being manipulative to get what she wanted, i.e. Papa and I to stay home. No such thing! She finally came to grips with it, but not before asking me, in a sad little voice, whether we would be back for her birthday. Since that happy event is in June, I was able to say with some certainty that we would.

We spoke on the phone every day of the three-day trip, usually more than once, Sara and Grandson Two and I. They filled me in on all the home front news, the really important stuff, like somebody threw up on the chair in the den and it was probably Obie but he's okay. The second night, as they were walking through the trees with their mother, on the way home after putting everybody to bed, Sara said,"I remember when Papa and I played basketball and he always loses because I cheat. We had so much fun." Yes, two nights ago, not ten years back. "And Gigi would come and lie on the bed with me and we'd watch PBS Kids. (Sigh.) It was so much fun. I miss them."

Meanwhile, in North Texas, I was thinking about how she feels when she hugs me so tight we both squeak, and I was missing all of them. When we got home next day, all was well. It took almost an hour for everyone to express how much we had been missed. Pogo, the Amazon, screamed for an hour, Muggles the cat, whom no one had seen since we left, spent a lot of time purring in Papa's lap, and Tess, the Frenchie, sat on me with a determined expression that suggested I wouldn't be getting out of her sight anytime soon.

It may be another six years before I leave again.

Infinite Diversity in Infinite Combinations

If you are or ever have been a Star Trek fan, you know what IDIC is. This is from the old Star Trek, born in the 1960's, the one where Captain Kirk and Spock and Bones boldly went, etc. The unlikely, entertaining, politically incorrect version, where larger than life characters tramped about the universe as ambassadors of goodwill, exploring new civilizations and blithely ignoring the Prime Directive whenever it suited them. In other words, being wonderfully, unabashedly human.

IDIC stands for Infinite Diversity in Infinite Combinations, a perfectly fascinating and viable premise in "real life". It would be incredibly boring if we were all stamped from the same mold, without individuality or quirks of our own, moving in lockstep toward some common, identical goal. Such a scenario would doubtless be desirable in the extreme to many segments of society; no dissention, no problems, no adaptations necessary. Just a calm, unquestioning acceptance of whatever dogma was presented, kind of like sheep moving implacably in the direction they're pointed.

Sometimes it seems like things are moving that way in spite of the eccentricities of human nature that make life interesting. But when you are allowed to look at people, to see who they really are, you find the differences that refresh your point of view and give you hope.

In a microcosm consisting of three grandchildren, IDIC is demonstrated every day, endlessly fascinating, revitalizing and frustrating by turns. Grandson One is a pragmatist, a skeptic, calculating his options with as much aplomb as any starship captain ever could. He is mechanically/electronically inclined, interested in the workings of things and how they all come together to run, or fly, or whatever they do. He sees how things work in his head in ways others could never imagine. That is the arena in which he is most comfortable; that is what he instinctively grasps and understands. It is logical, it is predictable, and it will not suddenly go to pieces on him and assert a will of its own, thereby upsetting his own particular applecart.

Grandson Two is a feeler, an empathizer, and a dreamer. He wants everything to run smoothly and be good, not just for him, but for everyone he knows or comes in contact with, and does everything he can to make that happen, often at his own expense. He can talk to anybody, friend or stranger, and has an innate skill at making people feel good. Inanimate things are not of much interest to him, though he has certain skills that will stand him in good stead. He loves the farm and the mundane sameness of it; the chores, the tractors, the animals and their behaviors. They are individuals to him and he is learning how to deal with their idiocentric personalities without taking it personally.

The boys were born one day apart. They share the same genes on one side, at least; they have been raised together. When they were babies, they had a "twin" language that only they understood. Now that they are growing up, their natural paths have diverged and they might as well speak different languages, so difficult it is sometimes for them to come to agreement.

Then there is Sara. She is from a different culture, one where women seem to be of little value and often repressed. She is irrepressible, full of joy and temper, the fire of life so bright it dazzles. Her mother remarks that she is not a "girly" girl, to which I say hurrah! She is far too busy to worry about frills and body image; she is using her wits and her limbs and her spirit to move her world in the direction she wants it to go. She never chooses books about princesses and beauty queens; her latest choice is a very good study of reptiles and insects. Not for nothing is her nickname "Ladybug". Digging in the garden is a favorite pastime; playgrounds are her delight. Tagging Papa about as he gets hay or moves cows or goes to the sale suits her as much as it ever did the boys. She has great friends at the barn, and birth and death are no strangers to her, young as she is.

A day or so ago, she was crawling through the fence to join me when Papa came down the drive with a young bull snake perhaps two feet long coiled around his arm. She was a bit wary, but excited at the prospect of holding it, so Papa showed her how to grasp it behind the head and by the body. She clutched a bit when its tail coiled around her arm, but Papa explained what it was doing and she relaxed. Her face glowed with pride and her dark eyes sparkled as her mom took pictures.

"I think those boys are afraid of snakes," she announced, one up in the ceaseless competition, "but I'm not."

Together they took the little fellow up to the hay barn, and she explained to me later how he slid off under the hay to catch a mouse. Fodder for show-and-tell, for sure.

Fingers In The Car Door – A Part of Growing Up

It finally happened, that most dreaded but almost inevitable accident that befalls little people at some time in their young lives; Sara's fingers got slammed in the car door. In the grand scheme of things, held up against hurricanes and tsunamis and the like, this is of microscopic insignificance. But if the fingers are tiny and tender and attached to someone you love, and they are smashed and bruised and swelling, for a little while nothing else is more important.

She cried,. holding her hand up piteously to Papa, who was fussing with ice in a zipper bag and trying to console her. She took turns in her mom's lap and Papa's lap and mine, and we all did that instinctive rocking thing you do with small ones, but it still hurt. We tried distraction, consolation, and Motrin, not necessarily in that order, but every time any of us looked at the cruel black lines on her little fingers we all felt bad again.

It happened to her left hand, which is the only good thing about it, since she is right handed and is heavily into writing just now. She was on her way to our house with her mom and Grandson Two and a cousin to have a hamburger at the end of a busy day when the door got slammed on her. Because she's small but also determined to keep up with the big boys, she's often in a somewhat perilous position. The ends of busy days are hard for everyone; when everyone is tired, distracted, and hungry, bad things can happen.

By supper's end the Motrin had kicked in and she had become a bit more cheerful, enumerating all the things she probably couldn't do with that hand and looking forward to telling her teacher and her friends about her grisly experience. She is not above milking a situation, and she does it well, but I'm too old for such drama so close to bedtime.

Drama is a way of life for youngsters. The Grandsons recently had some project going for which they needed cash. With several jobs that needed doing and a shortage of time, it seemed a fair exchange to me; cash for work. They made a strong appeal for a somewhat, shall we say, giftier situation, but we came to an understanding and they began to work on the tasks assigned.

First on the list was the chicken house. I needed the nest boxes cleaned out and fresh hay put in, with the stipulation that no matter how amusing it might be to see a hen jump and squawk when seized from behind, it was not to happen. Things went pretty smoothly until they came to the recently vacated nest of the broody Buff hen, now in a cage with her new-hatched chicks. Such a nest is usually a mess, a few unhatched eggs and a generally unpleasant aroma combining to create a situation messy by any standards. The boys came in with rolling eyes and snorts of "gross!", appealing to me to let them skip that one, leaving disgruntled at my smiling refusal.

They cleaned up the chicken pen with enthusiasm if not efficiency, which led to a couple of things being redone. They cleaned up the yard – mostly their stuff anyhow, but a big job – and hauled it all out to the trash. They watered the ducks and changed the goose water. Coming in with red faces and sweaty hair for a drink, they checked again on the price tag and agreed between themselves that they were working too cheap, an opinion unfortunately not shared by their employer.

At last all was done, money changed hands and they disappeared to make big plans. Only later did I find the disputed nest box still in its original unclean state; this will necessitate a revisitation of the henhouse, a fact I will apprise the workmen of this weekend. And there will be no bonus for the return trip, either. What were they thinking? That I wouldn't notice, or that I wouldn't call them on it? Ah, the optimism of youth!

Goodbye Jake

There is a quote from one of my favorite movies that says something like, "Hellos are most usually happy, goodbyes are most usually sad, but it's what's in between that counts". The grandkids have had more experience with all of that than many kids do because of their lifestyle. Animals are born and die as a matter of course, and the kids have been in on all of it from their earliest days.

Sometimes it strikes closer to home than other times, but as a rule they handle it well. Oftentimes they handle it better than I do. They have watched babies being born and delighted in their antics; they understand that sometimes babies die, and they feel badly. They have helped Papa bury everything from dogs to horses and in between.

Recently I bought Grandson Two a Nigerian Dwarf doe and her two 5-week-old doelings. Nigerians are dairy goats in miniature, probably weighing less than a good-sized Labrador. The babies are diminutive, adorable little bundles of energy. Being small, they are easier for children (and old folks!) to handle than the bigger versions. Sara was a bit piqued about the deal and announced that she didn't like goats anyway, though when her brother reluctantly agreed that she could help him with them sometimes she leaned against me, gave me the big brown eyes, and asked whether she might have one someday. I will let you draw your own conclusions about that one.

So far Grandson Two is rising early, tending his tiny herd before he goes to school, and seeing to their comfort when he gets home. He takes the doe out on a lead, babies scurrying to keep up with mom, to browse a bit in the evening. Being who he is, he worries about leaving them alone all day, even though the house and pen are sturdy. At his request, I go and check on them around noon. He is learning things already, adding to what he already knew, that will enrich his life in many ways. Not the least of his lessons is being responsible for something other than himself, something helpless and trusting that looks to him for food, protection and care. If there is a downside to the lifestyle, it is that often the animals we tend and share our lives with get such a grip on our hearts that when we must let them go the pain is intense. Goodbyes are hard.

Grandson One is dealing with a goodbye of his own. He has just lost an old friend and is grieving him.

Jake was a big old yellow dog with a little white on his head and chest and feet. Grandson One can't recall when Jake wasn't on the porch, because he joined the family before the Grandson was born. Jake has always been there, constant as the sun, his big ears pricked at the sound of the door opening and his brown eyes watching to see whether he's included in the activity. For the last couple of years, stiff with arthritis and hard of hearing, he hasn't been as active. Still, he was always there.

About 15 years ago a neighbor of mine, Lucille Lewis, called me to ask if I was missing a dog; she said "a real sweet young dog" had been dumped at her house. Neighbors knew I had a lot of dogs so they assumed any dog they didn't recognize was mine. They also knew that if it wasn't mine, they could probably talk me into coming and getting it so that it became mine. Our son was out of a dog at the time, and Jake came to live with him. Jake was about a year old and full of heartworms he had to be treated for, with big dark eyes and a sweet expression. For his whole life Jake was a good dog, and that's the best thing anybody can say about a dog. When our son added Molly to the family, the two dogs may have stolen the odd chicken, but such thefts were few. Jake enjoyed stolen goose eggs, taken home to be eaten at his leisure in his own yard, but overall his transgressions were minor and easily overlooked. Jake was a good dog.

Grandson One came home from school last Wednesday to the news that his dad and I had taken Jake to the vet and that he was pretty sick. He had a malignant tumor on his liver. Just the night before he had refused his dinner, and that day he didn't want to get up, so he didn't feel really bad for long.

Our son agreed with the vet that the time had come. He and Grandson One buried Jake in the yard under a tree. Even though I've lost so many in my lifetime, there isn't much I can say to a heartsick little boy.

A couple of weeks ago one of my old collies died quietly in his bed. My tiny little pillow partner poodle isn't doing well with his heart condition. These are things we struggle with; it just has to hurt until it feels better. I ignore people who say "they're just animals". They cannot have ever really loved a dog, though if they have ever owned one they have surely been loved and just didn't notice.

Hellos are usually happy. It's the goodbyes that make our hearts ache so. Goodbye, Austin. Goodbye, Jake. You were good dogs.

Sara Is Launched

The first moment I held Sara, eight months old and newly arrived from China, I fell madly in love with her. Even in that first rush of euphoria, I knew this dreaded day would come, and she would one day have to go to school.

A couple of years before Sara's homecoming, the boys went into kindergarten, but there were several big differences. They were big fellows, rough and ready to take on school, and I was, frankly, tired. Not tired of them, just tired out by them. There had been five years of twin language (now called "buddy" language), twin appetites, twin energy and twin capacity for thinking up new and ever more exhausting ways to get into mischief. Though they aren't twins, they were born one day apart and have always lived almost like twins. I was still involved in their lives, just not so intensely.

And Sara was here. She was small and delightful and school for her seemed far away. Pre-school was a pleasure, since she went three mornings a week and Papa or I took her and picked her up. There were donuts in the morning on the way to school, and Wednesday afternoons in the park with the ducks, or at the big playscape with a friend. There were late mornings with her on my lap and a cup of coffee, watching the chickens in the yard or Barney on TV. Afternoon naps and cuddle time and playing games made up our days, one after another. Papa took her to Lampasas with him to get feed and they always went to the park; she was known everywhere we went from the grocery store to the vet, and always elicited big smiles with her gamin ways.

Suddenly time telescoped in on itself and it was the last summer before she started kindergarten. All at once I thought of a hundred things I meant to do with her and hadn't, always thinking there was plenty of time. I had forgotten that there's never plenty of time. Suddenly, now, her baby days were done. She would brighten someone else's days, though never as much as she had ours. Talk turned to what school was really like, where she would go, what things she would need. Her mom and I went shopping for clothes with her and she was very particular, her taste in color quite different from her mom's. We found jeans that actually fit her long-legged, elfin body and bought five pairs. She chose shoes that light up with every step and some with glitter; Velcro closure for ease and shoestrings for the grown-up pleasure of tying her own shoes. She was set.

I tried to ignore how fast the days spun past; June birthday, swimming lessons, all the summer fun there was to be had in such a hot, dry year. We were busy, and I told myself everything was going just fine, which it was.

Except that last week I suddenly began to cry sometimes when I looked at her, and since I couldn't let her see me doing it, things were complicated. She was by turns excited and concerned about this new undertaking. "But who will help you feed the chickens and water the plants?" she asked more than once. "You know I love to help you, but I won't be here." Each time I told her that I loved her help, but she would be able to help me after school sometimes. It was plain that her mind was in the same place as mine; well and good, but it's not the same. Occasionally something would come up, like the feed trips to Lampasas, and she would say, "But I can't do that anymore. I won't be here." Clearly she was worried about our capacity to run things without her help.

Actually, so was I.

And then it was the night before The Day. Open House had been a mad scramble of parents and siblings and chaos. Sara had met a little girl or two, but knew no one. Still, she cheerfully packed her lunch and chose her shirt and shorts the night before, modeling each and every one for her adoring audience, Papa and me. She made her choice, which not surprisingly coincided with Papa's favorite, got her bath, and bid her goodnight. Almost before we got home she called

131

and said she didn't want to go, she wanted to stay here. I lost my misery in the fervent hope that she would change her mind with morning, that it wouldn't be hard for her.

At lunchtime her mom called and said that Sara had done well. She started to cry at first, but stopped, and the one time her mom had the chance to check on her, she was busily working away. At lunchtime she told her mom that she had three new best friends and things were good. Every day can't be smooth, of course, but at least the first one was.

Sara is launched. May her journey be a bright and marvelous adventure, the earnest wish of her watchers on the shore.

Chapter 6

The Four Leggers Are Better Centered

Heart Attack OK – Just Don't Hurt the Calf's Leg

Every now and then we are reminded that we are not everything we once were. Here I except the spandex bunch, which I hold in awed admiration, because they are probably more than they used to be. For the rest of us, it's easy to forget how time has altered our abilities in probably multiple ways. The changes are so subtle and we are so good at making accommodations that limitations go basically unnoticed most of the time. A little twinge here, a minor ache there, what's the difference? Instead of throwing the 50 pound bag of feed over one shoulder and walking off with it, we spend an inordinate amount of time finding the hand trucks to wheel it to its destination. It gets there all the same, regardless of the method of transportation, right?

It's only when a situation arises that is outside the normal operating procedures that we suddenly must acknowledge the fact that things – meaning us – have changed a bit. We must apply that old saw "work smarter, not harder" in order to get the job done. Unfortunately, this often occurs to us after we're in the middle of the situation and there's nothing for it but to see it through as best we can, hopefully learning something from the experience.

Buttercream is a beautiful cow, golden as ripe wheat, with great gentle eyes and a wonderful conformation. In the cattle world, she is a "10". Brighteyes Baby, her yearling heifer, is her exact image, just smaller. They are a joy to look at, together in the pasture. We enjoyed it so much that we forgot to check on mama's due date for her new baby and she sneaked one in on us; another golden heifer. Brighteyes was still with mom and still nursing, much to our chagrin. Obviously, a yearling will take every drop mom can put out and the new baby will, at the very least, not thrive. It was weaning time, ASAP and well overdue.

Coming home from town on the new baby's second day, we saw Buttercream in the pasture all alone, something that throws up a red flag. Cows are herd animals and don't generally graze alone unless they are about to calve or have already and are waiting to reenter the herd until the baby is a few days old. She was close to our son's driveway, not particularly interested in the slim pickings of the dry field. Driving up for a closer look, we found the new calf lying against the fence on the other side of the driveway from its mama. Clearly, she had parked it, moved into another pasture with the herd and now found herself separated from it by two fences.

We love these situations. In order to reunite the pair, one must be driven away from the other up the fence line to the nearest gate. This is true of cattle, goats or horses, all of which, being herd animals, are convinced that being driven out of sight of buddies is a sure way to disaster. They will run up and down the fence screaming bloody murder until they're ready to drop rather than walk fifty feet to the nearest gate and be instantly reunited with said compadres because it takes them in the opposite direction for two minutes. Guineas are the worst about this, but at least they will eventually become so distraught with their abandonment issues that they will take wing and fly over the fence, usually just before you succumb to the temptation to smack them smartly in the tail feathers by way of encouragement.

Cows, of course, do not fly. They pace and bawl. Eyes fixed on the adored baby being threatened by Papa, the man who usually feeds her every day, Buttercream was no exception. She wasn't going to be driven around our son's house to the gate; she was just going to bawl and make abortive attempts to get through the fence to the child she had parked and left in the wrong pasture. Recognizing from long and bitter experience that the cow would never cooperate, Papa turned his attention to the now thoroughly alarmed calf. She might have joined in the plan but for the fact that her mom was yelling all sorts of dire warnings at her and there was no way to get to the warm drink she needed for reassurance.

Perhaps, I said, you could lift her over the fence and we could get her into the pasture with her mom. (Okay, but he used to do that all the time.) He gave me a look, but he climbed through the fence and quickly found that she was a pretty stout little heifer, totally averse to being lifted, period, much less over a fence. He suggested that he hand her to me over the fence and then I could drop her into the other pasture, but I think he was kidding, in spite of his somewhat stressed expression. Too, he was getting pretty hot by then.

Ultimately, he hooshed the baby up the fence toward the gate some distance away while mama broke into a frantic run, bellowing every other step, to meet them. Her alarmed cries alerted the rest of the herd, cudding in the shade, and it must have been a slow day, because they all got up to come and see what was going down. Papa got the calf through the first gate and came across the small field yelling at me to open the gate into the big pasture, where mama and all the aunts and cousins were congregated, jostling each other for a better view. When they arrived at the gate I saw that he had the calf by one hind leg, making her go on three legs, which gave him lots more control with less effort. It didn't look too comfortable, though, and I remarked as I closed the gate behind the calf that I hoped he hadn't hurt her leg.

He leaned against the gatepost, wiping the sweat out of his eyes and catching up on his breathing while I latched the chain.

"Oh, good," he said, wiping his face with the tail of his shirt. "I can have a heart attack, but don't hurt the calf's leg."

Have you ever noticed how some people just seem to misunderstand half of what you say?

Boss and Lavender

This Place Is Smelly!

The autumnal equinox – the first calendar day of fall – has come and gone. Whoever is responsible for such things forgot to tell summer to go away. It's been hotter at midday lately than it was in August, way too hot to pursue strenuous outdoor activities – at least for me. But nature waits on no human's whimsical desire for more comfortable weather. She performs right on schedule, and the schedule is her own.

Dairy goats are seasonal breeders, and fall is the season. The bucks have been amorously inclined for a month or more, and it isn't hard to tell. They have musk glands on the tops of their massive heads, and those glands become active during breeding season. A lovesick buck smells quite a bit like a skunk that's been rousted by dogs and forced to defend itself. It's quite distinctive and carries over five counties when the wind is right, with heat and humidity seeming to make it stronger. Bucks also engage in a little practice called "marking". This involves rubbing their huge smelly heads on anything they can, including their handler. Back when I escorted many of the does to the proper pen where a lovelorn buck waited, my family could always tell.

"You've been playing with the bucks again," my daughter would say accusingly, turning up her nose at my malodorous clothes. "Just don't sit down on anything until you change, and don't put those clothes in the washer with mine!"

I had barn clothes I seldom wore anywhere else, but once in awhile I would be in a hurry to run an errand and forget my morning's activity. Heads would turn when I went into a store. The facial expressions ran the gamut from startled to stunned to horrified in about thirty seconds, reminding me of my unorthodox aroma. I'm sure people asked one another, "what do you think she does for a living?" more than once.

The does love that musky cloud, that almost visible olfactory aura surrounding the big fellows. Nature intended it that way, but then she has a funny sense of humor. After a doe has been in with a buck for a while, she doesn't smell so great herself, since he marks her as enthusiastically as he does everything else. That's why milkers aren't allowed anywhere near a buck until they've dried off.

Does will tell you when they are ready to be escorted to the breeding pen, and they are as individual in this as they are in everything else. One will stand against the pen fence while the suitor rubs his smelly head adoringly over her head and neck, babbling silly nothings in her ears. Her tail will "flag", wagging so hard it's just a blur. She will stand there all day and all night if you let her, not leaving even to eat and drink until the urge is gone. Another will stand at the pen and schmooze with the buck, but she won't miss any meals and if the sun gets hot, she'll wander off and seek the shade, leaving the lustful laddie calling after her.

Then there's the doe who drifts by the pen with a diffident air, a casual glance in the buck's direction, a mere suggestive flirt of the tail and she's gone. That's it. You have to be quick to catch it, or you'll miss her entirely.

And there is always the doe, every year, who chooses her own mate and refuses to be swayed by any other. The chosen buck's pedigree may as long as from here to the mailbox; he may always be tops in the show ring. The doe doesn't care what his papers are, or that you've been planning for kids from this breeding all year, or that the buck you chose for her is a grand champion and a knockout to look at. She wants who she wants, and it ain't him.

It's the young upstart in the back pen, the one you're not even sure you're going to keep. He's often not even the same breed and he's certainly not in her class, but I'm telling you, if she gets bred this year it will be that buck or nobody. She will fight and scream and throw herself on the ground and sulk and just in general be such a miserable wench that you will either just give in or skip her entirely. There are too many goats in the barn already anyway.

It's not a pursuit for the fainthearted or the delicate sensibility, but you get used to it. Unless you just don't intend to get used to it, which seems to be Sara's view. She gets halfway to the barn and stops and then, pinching her little nose between two fingers, announces, "This place is smelly! I'm going back to the house!" And she does.

Take that, Mother Nature.

Fudge, Floppy Ears and Precious

Georgetown may be having trouble attracting kids, but we never seem to have that problem. The difference is, ours are four-legged kids. Sara's friend Purple Rose of Cairo had her babies a few days ago and increased our population instantly by three.

Rose is a big black and tan Nubian doe, with a regal Roman nose and extremely long, fine ears. She was due on the 13th, but from the rapidly increasing size of her udder, I didn't think she'd make it. Sure enough, the one night we went out to dinner, she decided to domino.

Papa went up to the hay barn about 11:30 to deliver Freckles the calf her bedtime bottle and heard the unmistakable mother talk coming from the goat barn. When he checked it out, there stood Rose with two wet babies, looking slightly dismayed. He came to the house to get me, I grabbed some towels, and off we went.

Rose was moved from the community barn to a kidding stall, where she was destined to go the next day anyhow. It was clean and bedded deep with hay in readiness, but she had dropped her little ones into the dirt of the dry does' barn. Papa and I toweled off the two pretty kids and then went to the milk room to get the routine stuff to treat the newborns; iodine to dip navels to prevent entry of nasty bacteria into the little bodies and e coli serum to boost the natural immunity we hoped they got from mom.

Reentering the stall, we were astonished to find a third baby and a completely distraught mother. Rose has kidded twice before, one doeling each time. Here were three infants under her feet; each one was struggling to gain its feet and squeaky baby noises were coming from every direction. She had cleaned them all as they were born, but tending them all was freaking her out. She whirled this way and that at each new noise, touching each baby with her nose as if to reassure herself that this one, too, was hers.

I knelt in the hay and squeezed each teat gently to break the seal; Papa said the little belted doe had eaten and was smart about it, but the big gold buck had not. The third baby, a doeling, was still dopey and not ready to eat. As we held each baby to nurse, Rose nervously smelled their little wagging tails as if she thought we might have brought a ringer in to nurse. She pulled my hair gently and licked my face and hands, obviously ill at ease with so many children to look after. She looked into my face as if to say, what the heck has happened here? Are all these babies mine?

They all ate finally and curled down into the hay while Rose went from one to another, pawing them to get them up and anxiously chewing on their freshly dipped navel cords. We got her settled a bit, but every time one of the babies squeaked she whirled around to find it and half the time stepped on one of the others, causing it to cry. That brought her back around to check on it; meanwhile stepping on the one she had been looking at. It was pretty confusing for a while. Finally Papa snuggled them all under the little wooden kid shelter designed to keep anxious mamas from pawing babies all night and they passed out, tired from their introduction into the big world. Rose stood yawning, pawing half-heartedly now and then, and at 1:30 we went to the house, tired and satisfied.

Next morning she had it sorted out. They were all hers, not one kid splintered into three parts but three separate babies, and she is definitely up to the task of raising them.

Sara named them Fudge, Floppy Ears and Precious. Precious is the buck. When he weighs two hundred pounds and has some rather disgusting habits, we aren't sure Precious will seem as appropriate as it does right now, but what the heck.

Celebrities aren't the only ones who can give their babies goofy names.

Some Days I'd Be Happy With Manageable

It's not a perfect world, though that's what many of us wish for. Most days I'd be happy with manageable. Dealing with children and animals on a daily basis; I know to expect the unexpected. Letting down your guard is a surefire guarantee of disaster. The merest whiff of inattention, the barest breath of a thought remotely resembling "surely just this once it will be okay", puts the most natural among us on high alert.

Take dogs, for instance; and on some days you could take any number of mine without a whisper of dissent from me. Several dogs reside here, all sizes and dispositions. We know each other well. I take care of them as well as I can, and it's no small task. It is my job to lug big bags of dog food in, wash blankets every week, drag them to the vet when they need to go (the operative word here is drag), supply them with chew toys in a usually vain attempt to save the chair legs and just in general tend to their well being.

In return they give me companionship, unadulterated, unconditional love, endless amusement, monstrous messes and more general aggravation in a week than the population as a whole sees in a year. Especially during storm season. Or if a chicken flies into the dog yard or a cat walks past, or one of the dogs looks wrong at another one and they fall on one another like demented badgers looking for a death hold, or (my personal favorite) a gate is left one-half centimeter ajar.

Instantly the dog nearest the gate springs into action, making a leap that would qualify for the Olympics and shouldering aside anything in its way. That would usually be me as I make a desperate grab for ears, tail, whatever is nearest me, while shouting the dog's name in my most authoritative manner, which, of course, it ignores completely. Depending on who it is, it may pause for a microsecond outside the gate to give me a look of delirious joy that says, "Free at last! Free at last!" before bounding off in search of loose chickens, small rabbits or anything disgusting it can roll in.

Or the look may say, "I knew I'd break outta this joint sooner or later! See ya!". This one trots away with an unconcerned air, knowing only too well that its trot will serve to keep it well out of my reach.

Riggs is the latter type. He is a powerfully built, handsome heeler mix. He carries himself with grace and dignity and a sense of well-controlled power. While he never starts anything, he almost always finishes it. He and I are very fond of one another. I've had him since he weighed 5 pounds; he slept at the foot of the bed until he weighed 45 pounds and

Papa suggested a change of sleeping arrangements. Riggs can travel in a smooth single-foot gait, tireless as a marathon runner. He lives for an open gate.

He does not come when called. He comes when he's ready. Sometimes that's immediately, if your voice is pitched just right. Sometimes he decides that it's a lovely day for chicken chasing or marking every tree on the farm, and then he proceeds calmly to accomplish his goal. So it was with his latest escape. He targeted a white rooster and no cutting horse ever gave a more agile and brilliant performance. When he got close enough he would grab the rooster by the neck and flip it over in a body slam, holding it on the ground until I got dangerously near. Then he would circle around it until it got up to run and repeat the performance.

Sara was yelling at him, but I didn't bother. I was too out of breath anyhow. I did advise the chicken to lie still and play dead, but chickens are too stupid to take anyone's advice. After one particularly hard slam to the ground the chicken did lie still and Riggs lost interest. He circled out in the pasture, smelling smells and marking anthills; I walked over to the chicken, who was lying on its back with its yellow feet sticking straight up. When I got quite near it blinked at me, so I picked it up, tossed it into the goat pen and it ran off yelling, doubtless wishing to impress some hens with its narrow escape.

Riggs, meanwhile, trotted to the gate and stood looking at me, panting. "Aren't you gonna open this gate?" his face said. His buddy, Babe the Border Collie, waited just inside to jump him in retaliation for the adventure he had not bothered to share. I let him in, went into the house and got a drink, and sat down to try and figure out why I keep such aggravating dogs.

Or maybe I was just wondering again how the dog got to be smarter than me.

The Saga of the "Dixie Whacker"

If a poll had been taken among the doe herd when Dixie was a youngster, she would have been voted least likely to be a model mother. She was not especially popular with her herd mates and she didn't give a darn. Being raised in the house in a crate and bottle-fed from day one, she felt herself to be much nearer the human end of the spectrum than the caprine end, and therefore way up on the evolutionary scale. The rest of the doe herd was simply not relevant to her life. Her attitude was merely reinforced when I tried to introduce her into the herd so that she could learn to be a goat. Not one of the older does wanted to teach her anything except to keep her distance. They bashed her if she didn't.

She was irritating, loudmouthed and obnoxious, even for a youngster, but then she is half Nubian and I supposed the Nubian girls would recognize the traits they had in common and at least tolerate her. Not so. Apparently she carried the less attractive personality quirks to a new level so that even the most schizophrenic Nubian wanted nothing to do with her. To a doe, they expressed their displeasure with her by means both physical and psychological. Dixie was a forlorn little outcast.

151

Things change, and so did Dixie. She is now easily the biggest, stoutest doe in the herd and nobody gets in her way. When everybody else goes out to eat, she lingers around the yard gate just in case someone more worthy of her attention comes out to play. She has her own spot to sleep and seldom chooses to eat from the common trough. Dixie is a law unto herself and she likes it that way.

Sara fed her from a bottle when she was a kid, and played with her for hours. Sara knows how to deal with baby animals, and she was never rough or unkind with the little doe. However, Dixie swiftly grew heftier and Sara did not; the balance of power shifted ever so subtly right up to the day Dixie knocked Sara down with a well-placed butt of the head. Things were never the same after that. Dixie terrorized Sara to the point that Sara wouldn't go into the barnyard; the minute she opened the gate, here came Dixie, hackles standing up and head turned to the side, threatening her former friend. This didn't sit well with Papa, who does not expect to be challenged by goats and certainly does not intend for Sara to be hurt, so he fashioned a stout stick for Sara which she dubbed her "Dixie Whacker", and stood it by the gate. After a couple of times getting whacked in the ribs with the stick, Dixie stood with a sulky expression and watched; Sara had the run of the place again, as long as she carried the stick.

The day came when Papa was taking some young bucks to the sale and Sara tried to convince him to put Dixie in the trailer. "She's just evil!" Sara said, "and she isn't getting any better."

Then Dixie kidded. She had one huge, beautiful buck kid, which we named Rebel, and she was indeed a model mother. Her temperament didn't change; she was just as opinionated and difficult as ever, but she loved that baby. She had a lot of milk and was surprisingly cooperative about hopping up on the milk stand and being milked. I had expected a battle of monumental proportions, but no such thing. All we had to do was bring the baby along with her so that she could see and talk to him, and it was cool. When he was four months old, bigger than any of the other babies, and had to be put up with the other little bucks to be weaned, she made a bit of a fuss, but less than I had anticipated. She returned to the outside world and resumed her former life. Sara resurrected her Dixie whacker and life went on as before.

Five days ago one of the young does got into the pasture next door and Sara came to tell me that she couldn't get her back where she belonged. "She's my friend with the wobbles," Sara said, "and she's screaming and screaming because she can't get home." (By 'wobbles', Sara meant wattles, the small vestigial appendages goats sometimes have on their necks.) When we went out to rescue her friend with the wobbles, I spotted Dixie off to herself, lying down. She's been doing that a lot, since she was due to kid on the 7th and has been enormous for weeks. Her feet were a bit swollen, her tail ligaments had loosened, and her temper was incendiary to say the least. On closer inspection, I saw that she had produced a kid, all dried off and staggering around her head, and was well into producing a second. She had chosen a protected spot in a mud puddle, so she and the baby were already a mess. Sara went kiting off to get Papa and things rapidly got interesting. After the second baby came we got her into the kidding barn, cleaned everybody up and settled them in. Two pretty babies, a buck and a doe; Dixie was appropriately proud of them..

An hour or so later, doing various barn chores, I looked into her stall and found her lying down, pushing. Another baby? I hiked to the house for clean towels, told Papa what was happening, and off he went. When he arrived, Dixie was peacefully munching hay while on the ground behind her lay the third kid, still in the sac. She was ignoring it. Papa tore the sac off, slung it and gave it some chest compressions, all the while thinking it was no use, when suddenly it sucked in air. It is a big beautiful buck kid, and it is ours.

At present he is living with a gentle natured young first timer Alpine; she won't let him nurse but she allows him to sleep with her kids and doesn't try to kill him. Dixie slammed him into the wall every time he moved; it was as if she said, "I tried to kill him in the very beginning and you messed that up, so I'll do it now." He is on a bottle and thriving, poor motherless baby, while two stalls away Dixie sleeps with her head protectively across her other two children.

Sara's comment? "Gigi, why are you surprised? I told you she's an evil woman!" Out of the mouths of babes.

Walk softly and carry a big stick!

What Goes Up Must Come Down

Muggles spent the night in a tree. That would be totally unremarkable if Muggles was a bird of any sort, but he is a cat. Not just any cat, but an inexperienced, coddled young housecat. The tree was not just any tree, but one of the tallest, biggest elm trees on the place, smack in the middle of the dog yard where several big hairy cat-hating dogs reside. Muggles perched near the top of that tree and loudly proclaimed his plight to the world at large, interspersed with urgent pleas for assistance.

No matter that we had tried to shield him from the dangers of the world at large. He never believed us when we told him how good he had it, warm blanket on the foot of the bed, gourmet cat food always in the bowl, fresh water and toys and ear rubbing whenever he asked for it. Like most youngsters, he longed for adventure and the great unknown. His first foray into excitement came about two weeks ago, when he escaped his torturous confinement and was gone for two days and three nights. We searched and called and cried (well, one of us cried), but he was nowhere to be found. He turned up about 2:30 one morning, skulking in the bushes and complaining about how cold and tough it was all alone out in the dark, and was scooped up and taken in with much rejoicing and more tears.

That trip earned him a visit to the vet and several booster shots just in case, but he didn't learn a thing. This escape was a little less traumatic, since we figured he had gained a little wisdom. We obviously overestimated his ability to take care of himself. Our daughter remarked that he has never been the sharpest knife in the drawer; he has always spent time in front of the aquariums studying the fish, a perfectly acceptable pastime, except that after a few minutes of watching them, he makes a wild leap at the glass, clonks his head and falls on the floor. He has always fallen off the bed when in the throes of wild play and almost never lands on his feet, but that's a myth anyway. He's like an armful of limp spaghetti to handle, and hangs his head backwards to look at you upside down when he's in someone else's arms.

We put all that down to youth and exuberance. After this tree thing, though, we may have to rethink things.

In the first place, going into the dog yard demonstrates either a death wish or, at the very least, severe stupidity. He shouldn't have to be too smart to avoid four dogs, the least of which weighs 65 pounds, snarling and yelping at the fence designed to keep them in and keep out hapless individuals whom they view as fair game, which is almost anything smaller than 65 pounds and slow enough and dumb enough to come into their yard. Okay, since they sleep about 22 hours a day unless something interesting draws them to rave insanely at the fence, maybe they were all asleep in the kennel when he ventured in.

Somebody must have waked up. That's usually Dulce; there was probably an instant when she couldn't believe her luck, and that must have been the minute Muggles had to make it to the tree. He's never climbed a tree that I know of, so I'm sure he would never have scooted up the ten feet or so of straight trunk to the first big branch except under extreme duress.

Snapping fangs would qualify as duress. By now the other three big hairy beasts were probably awake, alerted by Dulce's delight at the possibility of the imminent destruction of an actual cat. So Muggles, anxious to avoid that possibility since the cat in question was him, went ever higher. And there he sat, safe from the threat on the ground, but terrified.

And there I found him hours later when I went out to feed late bottles to two goat kids living at present in the chicken yard. He began his terrified importuning the moment he heard my voice, but it took some time to locate him with the flashlight, way up in his leafy bower. I was instantly terrified, too. Bottle feeding suspended, which led to some outraged importuning of their own from the hungry kids, I raced inside to call in the dogs before Muggles fell out of the tree and into their mouths.

They were all asleep in the kennel, but obligingly followed me in, apparently having forgotten there was a cat in a tree in their yard. Maybe they never knew it, though I think I'd rather they had chased him up the tree; hopefully such an experience would cause him to steer clear of that yard in the future.

Dog dilemma solved, it became obvious that Muggles didn't know how to get down. Yes, I know, all cats climb trees, but they do it in small stages and learn how to back down. He didn't have that experience. Papa sat under the tree and called while I fed goat babies. Later I took over, wheedling and coaxing and listening to his plaintive wails and excuses and pleadings to come up and get him. Ling Ling, an old and seasoned tree-climber, sat patiently with me and I asked him whether he might go up and show Muggles how to get down. He gave me an amused glance and returned to washing his paws in a plainly disinterested and heartless manner.

At last, chilly and stiff and very tired, I had to go in. Muggles' frantic cries followed me and troubled what little sleep I got. About 5 a.m. I roused to see him walking up the bed to nuzzle Papa, his favorite, who had abandoned him to his fate far sooner than I had. He then crashed in the blanket, put his forepaw over his face, and checked out.

It's always easier going up than coming down, but the old adage is true. What goes up must come down. Even Muggles.

Owning A Horse Is Cheaper Than Buying Prozac!

Owning horses is rather like being responsible for very large, excitable, perpetually hungry, accident-prone and totally charming children. You must pay attention at all times to their body language, be very clear in your directions to them, and sometimes just get out of their way and enjoy them.

Horses belong to the prey class of animals; that is, they are eaten by the predator class. Prey animals have eyes located more on the sides of their heads, the better to see predators sneaking up intent on making them lunch, whereas predators have eyes in the front of their heads. Horses recognize this instantly; we are predators and probably up to no good. Humans must constantly reassure horses that indeed we wish them no harm and certainly do not intend to leap upon them and devour them. Mother Nature has programmed deep into their DNA the "yes but" factor; "yes, but just because you didn't do it yesterday doesn't mean you won't change your mind and do it today."

Many people, including some who make their living with horses in some way or another, think horses are stupid. You can't be stupid as a species and survive, the possible exception to that rule being the human race, which, incredibly, continues to survive its own stupidity.

Horses are flight animals; the thing they fear most is restraint since being unable to flee at least their perception of danger means disaster. Perhaps the danger is only a white bucket sitting in a place where there has never been a white bucket before, but everything is relative. It is advisable, when you're working with a horse, to learn to think like a horse and snort at a strange white bucket as if you think it might grab you by the ankle as you walk past. The horse will understand that you know a dangerous situation when you see it, and trust your judgement.

Horses thrive on routine and the sameness of things; if a gate is always open, you'd better show it to them if it is now going to be closed. A new fence should be marked with something light and fluttery every few feet to grab their attention and keep them from running through it. Hand walking them around a new pasture is an excellent idea and changing their environment is best done in the broad daylight to give them time to adjust. It also makes sense because when they do something completely horse like, the vet can work better in the daylight.

Ah yes, veterinarians. There are a good many excellent equine vets in this area. We know several of them well, but a few we have seen only in artificial light. There is a rule among horses that rolling on the ground in agony with that particular bellyache known – and feared – by all horse owners as colic is best done just after sundown and closing time at the vet's office. Too soon, and there will be no after hours charge. Too late, and you may die before morning unless you have the kind of ocd owner who has to see you standing quietly asleep just before said owner goes to his/her own uneasy rest. Ghastly accidents and bloody mishaps are acceptable at any hour of the day, since the owner is often not at home and will not discover the horse until feeding time in the evening, at which time panic and guilt will rise to a maximum level and virtually incapacitate said owner.

A healthy bank account is helpful to the horse owner. It's not easy to maintain a healthy bank account once you acquire horses, however. There is feed, hay, tack, buckets, hay feeders, halters and lead ropes, fly masks and an infinite assortment of equipment to make your horse more comfortable and you a bit poorer. You naturally want it all. There are training books and videos, workshops, books on care and feeding; fly spray and joint supplement, blood boosters and body conditioners, shampoo and coat conditioners, grooming tools like brushes and curries and sweat scrapers and hoof picks. The big guns use horse vacuums and automatic shampooers, hoof polish and face polish and clippers to trim up any loose hairs. There are blankets and fly sheets and leg wraps...the list is endless, depending on what your discipline is. It just adds up, no matter what, to a tad bit more than you had intended to spend.

Then there are vet visits, vaccinations, farriers, and dentists. Their appointments are more closely scheduled than your own doctor visits, usually set up on a regular schedule. For special problems there are equine acupuncturists and massage therapists, expert saddle fitters and bit specialists. Again, it all adds up.

Perhaps one of the most deadly expenses is the "potato chip syndrome". That is, once you own a horse, you periodically get the fever to own another. One is never enough for the true horse enthusiast. When the fever strikes, it is akin to the new car fever some people experience when new models come out; there is no peace until you acquire the object of your desire.

In the case of horses, that means more buckets, halters, fly masks, farrier visits, etc. etc. etc. It is actually illogical to be addicted to a hobby that is expensive, demanding, time-consuming and filled with so much potential danger and heartbreak. As a horse owner, you recognize this fact from time to time and vow to change your ways, cut down on the numbers and perhaps get out of the horse game altogether.

And then you walk out into the pasture and they come to meet you, great brown eyes shining, big, powerful bodies surrounding you, soft muzzles reaching for the treat they know you have hidden somewhere. Life and power pulse underneath the taut, sleek hide beneath your hand. Heat rises from them and their scent is intoxicating to you. The sound of their breathing, the little squeals and grunts they make, the quick, restless feel of them shifting around you is like nothing else in the world. When one of them drops his head against you and stands there, motionless in his trust, his will surrendered just because he wants to, your heart is healed from whatever has ailed it lately.

I highly recommend it over counseling, Prozac or any other artificial device man has come up with to soothe your unquiet mind. It only costs a little bit more. Well worth it.

Better than a Prozac moment!

Chapter 7

And There Has To Be A Miscellaneous Chapter

Don't Tear Off The Tag Off That Mattress Just Yet

It seemed as if Papa and I were aging really fast. We noticed it especially in the mornings, when we were almost too stiff and achy to get out of bed. Papa sat on the side of the bed for a minute or two before rising, but I just hobbled and groaned and moaned about old bones and stiff necks. We woke up a lot at night, too, trying to find a comfortable position. His back hurt all the time; my hip was sore and painful. We both had the same opinion of The Golden Years; more like Fool's Gold.

Our son mentioned once or twenty times that perhaps we should get a new bed. We smiled and nodded and privately thought that such discomfort could never be wrought simply because of a bed. How long had we had the one we slept on? he asked. Were we aware that beds did wear out? We smiled again, certain the bed was not that old, we were. It was not a comfortable thought. In fact, it was even more uncomfortable than the physical aspect of things.

We discussed doctors of various types, but that meant medications of various types, something we try to avoid. I can be nauseous, dizzy and sleepy all on my own without the help of the pharmaceutical companies, thanks a lot. I have a marked aversion to

169

medications that are supposed to fix what ails me this week and are recalled next week because – oops! – one small side effect they simply hadn't noticed is death. So sorry. Yes, it's paranoid, and they have a pill for that, too, but I don't take it. So, no doctors.

Then we had occasion to be out of town overnight and the motel sported a bed that was big, smooth and very firm, something we noted as we deposited our travel-weary carcasses on it. We didn't wake up until morning, arising with a tenth of the usual effort. Waking up at home the next morning as stiff and painful as usual, we remarked about it. Perhaps we weren't yet as old as we'd feared. Perhaps our son – could it be true! – was right.

Came the day we were in a shopping center and impulsively entered a mattress store. Papa was drawn by the sale signs festooning the windows; I followed him because it was too hot to sit in the car. He was seeking the mattress we had slept on in the motel. We had pulled the covers loose and written down the information on a little piece of paper, which was, of course, no longer in our possession. Papa thought he remembered what it said. He discussed the merits of various mattresses with the eager and knowledgeable young salesman while I gingerly stretched out on first one and then another, feeling far too foolish to know what any of them felt like. We took the young man's card and departed.

A week or so later we bought a bed. Immediately
second thoughts assailed me. We had slept on our
old bed for a very long time; all the grandkids had
napped there, eaten popcorn there while watching
the Disney channel or Power Rangers, bounced on
it until they were so big their heads threatened to hit
the ceiling and curled up cozily under a blanket to
read with me. Sara still did all those things. I wasn't
sure I wanted to discard it as if it meant nothing,
sore neck or not.

On the delivery day I had to be somewhere else,
but Papa was home. The delivery truck which
arrived in the midst of a tropical downpour could
easily have held a whole houseful of furniture – and
did, for all we know. Our driveway is not made for
such vehicles and there was a brief period of
consternation, but they finally got down to moving
the mattress and box springs into the house, ducking
under dripping grapevines and dodging wet wisteria
tendrils to make it to the back door while various
dogs, confined for the event, shrieked intruder alert!
at the top of their lungs. The transfer was
completed, the new bed installed and the old one
headed for that great bedroom in the sky. It was
probably time; turns out we bought it in 1978.

My first look at The Bed came a bit later. A
bedroom is smaller, more intimate, and in our case
more full of stuff than a showroom. The Bed looked
huge and taller than I remembered. Incredibly,

impossibly tall. I tried to sit on it, and couldn't boost up that high. The only way I could manage was by means of a fierce lunge, followed by a less-than-graceful scramble, winding up somewhere in the vicinity of its poufy, pillow top center. Once ensconced up there, it felt like I imagine it might feel to be perched in a howdah on the back of an elephant about to rise. Somewhere below me on the floor, Tess the Frenchie and Rocky the Shih tzu sat staring up at the insurmountable obstacle to their heretofore-comfortable sleeping arrangement. I couldn't see them, much less lean over and scoop them up. When I slid to the edge of The Bed, I couldn't touch the floor. I dangled. It wasn't what I had bargained for. Sara announced that it would never work. "Come and look," she said indignantly. "No bounce. Can't they bring the old one back?"

But the new one slept great. Once I hoisted the dogs up and got in it myself, it was comfy. I did find myself rolling to the side, as if the center went uphill, but I thought it was my imagination. I worried about the dogs jumping off of it and tried to avoid that, but otherwise I was getting used to it and beginning to feel a bit like one of those Victorian ladies ensconced in a vast, rippling sea of sheets and pillows. Since we did feel better in the mornings, I thought it might be okay. Perhaps I could find some kind of stepstool for the dogs and myself.

There was a 30-day trial period before making it final, said Papa. It can be changed for a shorter one, without the poufy pillow top, he said. "And I want to", he added. Turns out he was dangling a bit as well; being six feet tall he wasn't accustomed to having his feet not touch the floor when he sat down. He had no plans to become so accustomed. The poufy thing bothered him, too.

The thing is, the second mattress isn't all that great for either one of us, for a whole different set of reasons. It's certainly a no-go with Sara, who says this one has no bounce either. Hmmm. Wonder where they took that old bed?

But I Didn't Call 911!!!

Everyday life on the farm can be challenging, exhausting and downright depressing sometimes, especially when we hit a long stretch of bad weather. Cold weather is terrific up to a point, but dreary gray days, mud that sucks our boots off, miserable livestock, dwindling hay and shrinking bank account do not a happy farmer make, any more than blistering sun and drought. We faithfully attend to the well-being of animals in our care when all we want to do is pull up the covers and sleep until spring; it makes some of us a bit testy. Living with a person who thinks 35 degrees is shirt-sleeve weather further strains the nerves. Often, for example, I am out swathed to the eyebrows in jackets and hoods and gloves, dragging boots weighted down with black mud through more of the same to get to the water faucet to fill chicken water up, my fingers screaming red and my nose numbed by the north wind. It doesn't do much for my temper to have Papa sail past in short sleeves with sweat on his brow and blithely ask, "Are you cold?"

In the house, while I am cooking up a storm just to stay warm and he is still in his short sleeves, I have contemplated actual bodily injury perpetrated upon him when he says, "Are you warm enough? Can I turn off the stove now?" No matter that the cats are lined up as close to the stove as they can get and the dogs, those not wrapped in their blankets, are lying against the radiator heater in the office. If he builds a fire without my having pitched a fit for one, it's a signal that the house must be approaching polar temperatures, and I add another layer of clothes. He sleeps with the covers thrown back, while on the other side of the bed I have added a blanket or two. Tess the Frenchie, Rocky the Shih Tzu, Milo the big yellow devil cat and I are bundled up together underneath it all. Sometimes I swear I can see my breath frosting in the air.

Add cold rain and north wind to such a night and the thought of cows standing out in the weather makes me even colder. I don't know how the people in Montana do it, but hopefully they all wear coats when they go out into the snowdrifts to look for their cattle.

Being a bit stressed by the winter weather as well as chronically electronically challenged, the necessary acquisition of new cell phones came at a rather bad time. We liked the ones we had, but the plan changed or some such thing and the old phones had to be replaced. The old phones were familiar, and I could work them with ease, speed and a fair degree of accuracy. Papa tried to get new ones as close to the old ones as possible but, alas, they are nowhere near the same. They look similar in size and shape, but there all similarity ends.

The number buttons are beveled and hard to punch. The key lock doesn't always work at first and must be redone, a fact brought home when the thing beeps merrily away in my purse, operating with an agenda of its own and quite possibly dialing the island of Maui, where I wish I had close relatives or dear friends, but do not. The menu is totally confusing and the directory inaccessible, at least to me, at least so far. There are five speed dial numbers I can use and heaven help me if I need to call somebody else.

For the first couple of days we had them, we recorded everything. Not because we wanted to, but because we couldn't figure out how to make the darned things stop doing it. There is a manual for them, written in several languages. Unfortunately it remains unclear whether any of those languages is English; it hasn't been of much help so far.

The last straw was New Year's Eve, when we had ventured to our daughter's house to eat a little chili and spend the last lively hours of the old year with grandchildren. As the hours advanced, we were all like a bunch of puppies with full bellies and had to keep jostling one another awake, but we did see the New Year in, more or less. Just as we arrived home and stepped out of the car, Papa's phone rang. "I don't have an emergency," he said, and then repeated it. A couple of minutes later he convinced the dispatcher at the 911 end of the conversation that he had not dialed his phone, which indeed was locked and should not have dialed at all. She was not pleased, and I don't blame her, and neither was he. That's no laughing matter.

The phone, however, that rascally little prankster, must see it differently, since it has repeated the gaffe a couple of times. The manual identifies this as a new feature; if I hit a certain number and don't follow up with more numbers, the phone is cued to dial 911 for me, presumably to aid in my rescue from whatever dire fate has befallen me. Since I don't know what number not to hit, I live in a heightened sense of awareness when handling the phone.

Our son spent almost an hour one day walking me through all the great features and wonderful qualities this phone has. He can almost make it speak in tongues. He then listened politely to my protestations that I don't want any of that stuff to happen, I just want to be able to get a phone call and make a phone call. Just a plain phone call. He shook his head and said sadly, "Mom, I don't think you can get that any more".

And now we have a new computer. The phone thing is small potatoes compared to that. Looks like a long winter.

Sometimes Having Is Not So Pleasant A Thing As Wanting

There have been several weeks of chaos and disintegration of daily activity in the house while Papa tiled floors, a long-discussed and much desired event. Admittedly, I campaigned for it ardently more than once. I was, as usual, naïve about the process, seeing only the end result. There's that old saying, "Be careful what you wish for", and my personal favorite, which Star Trek aficionados will readily recognize as a quote from Spock, "Sometimes having is not so pleasant a thing as wanting". Not that I don't want the floors tiled, they are finished now and it's everything I hoped for. I just don't want any more of the project, which has now expanded to include a coat or two of polyurethane on the paneled walls, i.e. most of the house. Of course it needs doing, and of course it looks very nice when it's finished and yes, it should have been done years ago. Let me think; we didn't do it because it involves a lot of mess, a horrible dose of noxious fumes and removing all of the doors on all of the kitchen cabinets. That's where we are now.

Meanwhile, if you lay anything down in the house smaller than a hay bale, you may never see it again. I'm tempted to wear my car keys around my neck, since they have a habit of disappearing under the best of circumstances, but they have that stupid big black clicker thing on them and I don't want that hanging on me. My desk is stacked at least a foot high, and when I get a minute to work on cleaning it off, there's nowhere to sort stuff. I have boxes of stuff to throw out, boxes to donate, and boxes that I want to keep – I think. On days when I just can't make one more decision, my frustrated loved ones are prone to say, "toss it!". They are probably right.

It rained and I couldn't find an umbrella. There was one in the car, but I was in the house. I just got wet; it was easier than searching for an umbrella. Both sets of keys to the car were, shall we say, unavailable for about six hours, which was pretty scary. For six hours, more or less, I was without wheels. Did you know that it costs about a hundred dollars to get replacement keys with that clicker thing on them? My cell phone was incommunicado for almost a whole day. I'm thinking that the stack of clean laundry it was under could have muffled its ring. Sara's mud boots are missing, but I don't think that has anything to do with the general disorder around here; they go missing pretty often. What really worries me are all the things that are missing that I don't even know about yet.

Several times a day I stop and practice gratitude. Perhaps one shouldn't have to practice being grateful for one's blessings, but I think it's human nature to become so focused on what's out of whack that we forget the good things about our situation. I'm grateful that we have a good, solid house of our own and that nobody wants to put a highway through the middle of it – yet. I'm grateful that we can tile the floors and paint the walls and fix things up, and that Papa is both willing and extremely capable. Most things that get lost turn up sooner or later, and are appreciated all the more when they do surface. Personally, I think there's a place where lost things hide until you stop looking for them, and then they reappear. I've found too many things in places where I swear I've looked a half dozen times before without success.

Meanwhile, in the midst of all the chaos, life goes on exactly as it pleases. Spring is spring, and Mother Nature doesn't care whether there are doors on the cabinets or not. Babies will be born and plants will need to go into the garden and animals will need to be tended just the same. The world has turned lush and green overnight, and every rain enhances the growth of leaves and grass. The cows don't hang around the hay bale every minute any more; they're down where the oats are finally growing, just when it's time to plow them up to plant new graze. Madison, the Jersey, has a big brindled daughter who recently calved; one of black bull's last children. It's no bigger than one of the dairy does, spry as a cricket and black as the inside of a pocket. Its mom puts it down while she goes off to eat and it lies, head down, without moving till she gets back. All you can see is its ears twitching now and then. After supper, when the cubes are all gone, the cow is off, walking like a woman in a hurry, tail switching. Now and then she lets out a low crooning sound, and as soon as she gets close enough to hear, up pops the little head and before you know it the calf is underneath her, filling up on warm milk. It looks around, foam dripping from its face, and then runs in circles around her, little tail stiffly upright, bucking a couple of times from sheer joy in life. Sara is enchanted with it and is trying to come up with a proper name.

She's also working on names for the baby goats in the nursery barn; almost every evening she visits them. They lose a lot of their appeal when they get big enough to knock her down, but for now they are small enough to cuddle. Nothing on the farm is as much fun to watch when they really cut loose to play; time ceases to shove you and worries dissolve in the pleasure of their wild antics.

Working in the house may strain my patience and endurance and make me too cranky to stand myself, but going outside in the new, green world of spring restores my equilibrium. Works every time.

Some Can Deal With Endings

We are clearing out my parents' house. It's time, and it has to be done, but it is a task I shrink from. I have been putting it off for several months, unable to face the final dissolution of all their worldly goods. Not that there are that many, or that they have any value whatsoever to anyone but me. It's the utter finality of it, I suppose. Once the house is emptied and the stuff is gone, it's finished. They are truly and forever physically out of my life. Some people deal very well with endings, but I never have, and getting older, with all the endings that implies, hasn't helped one bit.

There are a few absolutes which must be faced by everyone, no matter what your race or faith or financial position in life. The death of one's parents falls into that category. These are the people who brought you into the world, nurtured you in your youth, supported you in your journey into adulthood and delighted in the person you became. Theoretically, at least. For most of us the truth lies just a bit to the south of all that, but they are your parents, for better or worse, good or ill, warts and all, and somehow you all rub along in life together as a family.

At the very least they are always there in the background, a force to be reckoned with, no matter how you choose to deal with them. When the chips are down, they are most usually on your side against whatever adversity the world tosses your way, and when they are gone there is suddenly a great gaping hole in the fabric of your life. Chances are, before that happens there has been a dramatic reversal in the roles you all play in the family dynamic; gradually you become the nurturer and they are the nurtured. It's often far more difficult than dealing with your children, because your parents are not your children. They have just begun to behave as if they were, and to need you as if they were, and to resent the whole scenario, resisting the very help they need.

At any rate, with my father gone and my mother lost in the unimaginably dreadful labyrinth of Alzheimer's, it is time to clear out their house. How simple that sounds, and how painfully difficult and complicated I am finding it. I have received very good and well-meant advice from many quarters, which boils down to: call the Salvation Army truck to come and haul it off. Ultimately that is what will happen, but before that there is a houseful of personal things to be dealt with. No charitable organization wants love letters between a couple who were together from the ages of 16 to 87. Bank records, correspondence between friends and family, literally hundreds of cookbooks and recipe collections from my mother's kitchen, records (yes, actual vinyl 'platters' as they once were called), books, and pictures, pictures, pictures. All of that must be sifted through for the priceless keepsakes before the rest is consigned to the trash box.

I can't get far before I begin to cry. Someone else weeds out the inessentials for me. Unfinished business, personal issues, or just plain nostalgia for a time now gone when life felt simpler, safer and more pleasant, who knows? This is just something I'm finding it hard to do. A pair of faded denim shorts at the bottom of a box instantly conjures the memory of hot summer days when my mother stood in the kitchen barefoot, wearing those shorts and a pullover, happily making lunch for all of us. She did love to cook. A book of patterns for woodcrafts evokes my dad in his striped overalls, working in his woodshop to make the rocking horses all the great grandkids loved. A patterned bowl my mother liked to serve salad in, the Franklin Mint cars my dad collected when he got older, scarves she wore when she dressed for church, and those striped overalls…they all make me cry.

I know people who pack it all up and dispose of it swiftly and efficiently, a task begun and done. They never open the envelopes with their elegant script and begin to read the lives now ended; it's finished, they say, and has nothing to do with them. All the stuff is just that…stuff.

Perhaps that's true. Perhaps I've just been hiding behind that stuff, feeling that if it all stayed just the same, one day I'd walk in and there they would be, Mother on the couch and Dad sitting at the table reading the paper. But I won't. On the day we took my dad to the hospital for the last time before they went into the nursing home, while we were waiting for EMS to get there, he looked around the familiar room and then at me.

"I don't guess we'll ever be home again," he said, and broke my heart. Though I told him I thought they would, I knew he was right. Now all that's left to do is finish up and close the door at last.

The Green Hour Has To Be the Equal of Quality Time

Most of the time I just let the world go its own way. Any influence I might have on the way things work would be so infinitesimal as not to be worth the effort it took to exert it. To imagine it could be otherwise would be egotism at its finest. There is a modicum of influence to be had where my own small sphere is concerned; quite enough, in fact, to satisfy me and even stretch my somewhat limited energy. The inability to influence events on a wide scale doesn't preclude my desire to do so when I become aware of something that needs influencing. My frustration level quickly reaches maximum velocity and I have been known to stomp around the house venting in a loud and angry voice. This upsets the pushface pack, the members of which, if they are not immediately guilty of some heinous crime like pinning the cat against the wall and trying to lick his ears off, are certainly guilty of some past misdemeanor and tend to drop their ears and look penitent when our voices rise. For that reason I seldom watch the news or even read headlined stories in the newspapers; I am simply too opinionated.

But here's one too good to ignore. Great balls of fire! The "experts" who spend their time figuring out how to raise America's children have come up with a real gem this time. It's called "the green hour". That's right, they have decided that kids today don't spend any time outdoors, so there is now a book on the subject. Written to guide parents on how to induce their offspring to spend time out of doors every day, it involves – are you ready for this? – spending time outdoors with the offspring. Take nature walks, that kind of thing.

How about just walking into the room where the kid is thumbing the video controller, shutting off the system, and saying, "Go outside and play"? Too simple?

Having said that, I would not allow my grandchildren to do what my children did from simple fear that I would never see them alive again. One of the mysteries of life in today's society is the proliferation of really weird and creepy people who prey on the helpless, and children definitely fall into that category. Still, for town dwellers, sending kids out to play in the back yard remains doable, I think, if you have a fence with locked gates, a big loud dog and a watchful eye. Nosy neighbors would be a definite plus here.

On the farm, it's different. Green hours abound. There are fields and barns and thickets and a compost pile the size of a small foothill, all fenced away from the road and patrolled by watchful dogs. There are animals to be tended and grass to be cut and any number of projects to be done. One summer the grandsons spent a couple of weeks in earnest labor constructing two colossal chairs out of lumber dragged up from somewhere. In spite of the fact that one bore absolutely no resemblance to the other, they painted their names on the backs of the giant things. I never saw them sit in either one of those chairs; sitting wasn't the point. Building them was the point.

Sara rides her bike all over the place, as the boys once did and still sometimes do. They all swim in the pool in the front yard, observed by Rio the Arab, who would very likely join them if he could only figure out how to get in. They are trailed everywhere by Libby the Red Heeler and Janna, the big blonde Lab who is always ready for a belly rub or a thrown stick. There is a tank where the boys have been a few times, though the incidence of snakes is higher down there, fostering an attitude of caution on the part of the adults. Sara learned from Papa how to eat honeysuckle blossoms and pick peaches and plums in the orchard, and she likes to go to the garden with whoever is going that way. New baby anything is a natural draw for her; kids, chicks, goslings, peacocks. She bounces out the door saying, "I'll be in the yard, Gigi", and that covers some territory. Grandson Two helps out with goat chores; he knows the kids by name, who gets a bottle and what to feed each pen.

A "green hour" every day seems ludicrous to me. How can you plan that as if it was a special event? It ranks in my mind right up there with "quality time", that mythical period parents are advised to spend with their children every day. Of course, I'm an old lady; I remember when kids played outside because we wanted to, without fear on anybody's part and with a great deal of imagination. We built roads in the dirt with old hoe blades, Papa for his cars and I for my horses. We dug holes and filled them up, rode bikes with wild abandon, played cowboys and Indians and wild horses and furious games of tag/dodgeball/hideandseek/redrover. We swung on swings our dads made of rope with board seats and hung in trees in the yards, and soaked each other with the water hose in those rare summers when drought restrictions didn't apply. We got hot and sweaty and flopped on the concrete porch in the shade with big glasses of ice until we cooled off and then we went at it again. The days stretched into long, dusky evenings and we chased each other around on the hot asphalt under the streetlights until that final call in that certain voice ended the play. Nostalgia makes it all seem perfect; common sense says it couldn't have been, but I do believe we were lucky to be children in that golden time.

And I'm pretty sure I know what tack my granma would have taken regarding fitting a "green hour" into my day. I believe she might have said, "If she needs a green hour, maybe she could hang this load of clothes on the line. And the flower beds need watering while she's out there."

You can't get much greener than that.

Grandson Two and Jacque

Diversity Personified

At least some of us believe that we have made real progress in the area of diversity. As grandparents we are extremely proud of our Sara, whose birthplace was the mainland of China. Her glossy black hair and luminous dark eyes, not to mention her enchanting little face and quick mind, are a perpetual delight. There are those, we know, who do not approve. We are sorry for their unenlightened status, considering how much they must miss in the world.

In the real world, the natural world, such diversities are not uncommon. The most recent example resides in a big cage in our barn right now. Spring is Mother Nature's most fertile time. Just now we have about eight mother hens with chicks, each batch numbering from 3 to 11. They do their chicken thing naturally and efficiently.

Then we have an exception, an example of diversity. In our big hay barn, a petite game hen adopted an egg roughly half her size. She gamely did her sitting thing with careful attention. What must have been going through her small chicken mind as she guarded that monolithic egg day after day? Ultimately she hatched a fluffy yellow youngster of which she is exuberantly proud.

Imagine a young, petite mother giving birth to an offspring half her size, with a large black bill and

191

huge webbed feet that in no way resemble her own tiny, well-defined, slender yellow legs and feet. It also has a strange, loud voice rather than a thin, piping cheep. "Good grief!" she could have thought. "This can't possibly be my baby! He must have been switched at birth!"

No such reaction with the game hen. She could not be more proud. There seems to be no communication problem. The gosling eats when she encourages it, takes refuge under her woefully insufficient wing when tired or chilly and makes kind of strange and goofy sounds in response to her motherly clucking. She seems confident that the not so little one will soon learn to speak in chicken. After all, children develop at their own speed.

A complication: geese know a gosling when they see and hear one, and they definitely recognize this baby as a gosling, obviously stolen by this devious and evil upstart hen. At least one goose and gander pair stand guard at all times around the cage just in case the trap is sprung and the youngster escapes.

Said youngster has no thought of escape, being safe and secure with its mama. Obviously there is heartbreak ahead for more than one player in this custody game. The gosling will eventually grow up, seek out water, and ultimately choose its natural species. Mama will hatch again, hopefully more nearly her own species, but who knows? She obviously can love any child.

I keep saying, we can learn a lot by just watching animals and, in this case, birds. Love isn't dependent on size or shape, color or gender; the ability to love is a gift and open to infinite diversity. Even a little game hen knows that.

Sara and best friend Elizabeth

Eggs In My Pocket

Chapter 8

Nostalgia

I Think I Growed A Muscle Today

Spring is a time for new beginnings. Time to get busy with all those projects you planned on cold, dreary evenings by the fire. It's time to get out the lists, assemble the necessities and get started making dreams realities.

Ever notice how the planning is a lot of fun and the actual execution can be, shall we say, less than enjoyable? For one thing, during the planning stage you're sitting comfortably curled up with a pencil and paper and a cup of something cheerfully hot near at hand to sip on. Nothing is being born or, having been born, is hungry. There is no agenda created by someone else being waved urgently in your direction. Time is endless or at least expansive and all things seem not only possible, but simple.

The bitter truth is that when it comes time for the actual work to begin, an interesting number of events will have occurred. First and foremost, the help you counted on and were assured of when plans were being made has, to put it baldly, evaporated, drawn in a totally different direction by other pursuits or suddenly convinced that this is an ill-conceived idea and it would be best not to get involved in it. This is not good. You have made ambitious goals, which are pretty much unattainable alone. Okay. You scale the project down a bit. Not perfect, but doable.

Except that the materials you had planned to use are (a). out of stock but will be drop-shipped (whatever that is), by July 15, when it will be hot enough to roast a pigeon on the bare roof and you will definitely not be outside, (b). available, but will require a bank loan only marginally smaller than the one on your house to purchase or (c). nobody at any retail store ever even heard of what you're talking about, regardless of the fact that there are full-color glossy ads in the newspaper stating quite the contrary, but here is something just as good, nay, better than, and only a bit more costly. The only catch is, it's the wrong size, the wrong color, and not what you want.

You have choices here. Give it up, which is the swiftest, cheapest and probably wisest option. Go on to something else, like reading everything on the New York Times Best Seller list before it changes or trying to follow the political scene for longer than fifteen minutes before falling asleep or breaking your good china in rage and frustration.

Or back your ears, grit your teeth, and dive in. That's usually the choice around here. The second step in the project is improvise and compromise, two things at which Papa excels.

Having planted grass for three years straight in front of the house and seeing it deteriorate into a sea

198

of bare dirt/mud every time because of the dense shade, Papa decided this year to make the area into one big, free-form patio. No biggie. Get some big flat rocks from the big flat rock place along with some sand and smaller polished rocks for the spaces between the big rocks, dig out the hard black dirt, level it all out, lay everything down and there you have it.

In theory. In practice, the estimated cost of doing it perfectly made him sit down on the side of the trailer for a while, looking stunned. Only the fact that the boys were with him and they don't sit down quietly for long roused him to consider alternative measures. With his usual swift capacity for adaptation, he improvised, compromised, and hauled home the rock while a dump truck brought sand and smaller rock to be dumped in the driveway up close to the house, just about where we usually park cars.

The piles of sand and rock were greeted by children and puppies and Dixie, the goat kid, like ice-cold lemonade on a sizzling summer day. A sizeable amount got spread around and tracked into the house before the work ever began. The boys were recruited for hard labor and went to it with a will and, it was later revealed, an awesome appetite that had to be satisfied every couple of hours. Sara found her niche as overseer and critic and spring break week went well, as did the work.

It's shaping up. It's going to be fine. In fact, Papa went back for more rock to make a place for the lawn swing and chairs and stuff. Who needs pesky grass anyhow?

On the first evening after a day of shoveling and carting big flat rocks from thither to where Papa wanted them, Grandson Two was sprawled on the couch at home, grit in his teeth and sand sifting out of his clothes. Grandson One was in a big chair, similarly quiet for once.

"I think I growed a muscle today," Grandson Two announced, rubbing his sore arm. "It sure feels like it."

"Yeah," Grandson One agreed from his slouch. "Me, too. I hate when that happens. It hurts, don't it."

Meanwhile, back at the ranch, Papa was having similar feelings, though he didn't put it down to having "growed a muscle". It was more like pulled a muscle for him.

Now if I can just get all that sand out of the house...

The Promise of March

March is a great month. Spring appears on the calendar in March. Temperatures range from almost too warm to nighttime snappy, and the world is beginning to stir out of its winter sleep. Babies are everywhere; calves and lambs and kids are in almost every pasture. Something inside you gets a fresh start when you see a bunch of baby calves all stretched out in the sunshine with the big sleek mountain of their black daddy bull lying right in the middle of them, babysitting. Or watching them play King of the Mountain on the compost pile, running up and down it with their little tails stiffened straight up over their backs, sporting tufty little flags on the ends. They chase one another and bawl in hoarse, croaky calf voices while their mamas tear off the new grass nearby and keep watch to see when cubes are forthcoming.

New kids bounce around the nursery pen as if they had bellies full of bedsprings, chasing and jumping and kicking up their heels and sliding to a stop to look around with startled expressions that say, "how did I get way over here when Mom is way over there?" One small sound from her and they're off again, flying to her side to stick their heads underneath her for a quick nip.

The wild plum trees are in bloom and no perfume made by man is sweeter than their heady scent. They turn overnight from spindly, scrawny, dark brown twiggy skeletons to fragrant clouds of pure white bloom filled with the hum of hungry bees. The sun brings out the scent; at midday it's almost like a drug if you stand directly under the tree. There are wild plums all over the countryside, snuggled up in the groves of oaks, peeking out of stands of cedar, dipping their toes in the swift current of creeks. The plums we have on the place always put forth an impossible froth of blossoms, but never put on a single plum for all the bees' endeavors. It's the same with the wild peaches, which are not as numerous.

On the ground the wild blackberries stretch out new vines studded with small white flowers that later on become juicy berries, nowhere near as big as the domestic varieties but super tasty.

It's a great time to put on boots and check out pastures where we haven't been for awhile. I love old wooden gates hung on railroad ties that look like they've been there forever, probably because they have. I like fencerows crowded with wild roses and wild plums and blackberries and brambles because they are home to myriads of tiny birds and rabbits and whatever else needs a hidey-hole. It tickles me to watch the tiny birds with beaks stuffed full of grass flitting from branch to branch looking for the perfect spot to build a nest. I spike handfuls of dog hair combed from the collies' undercoats onto a tree branch and watch it pulled off by the thimble full to line a cozy home for nestlings.

The hens are laying double time. When I go outside they rush towards me like a feathered tide, their feet dry on the stones in front of the house. They watch me expectantly, all appetite, to see whether I've brought them goodies from the kitchen. I put a tray of young lettuce in the wheelbarrow to water it and when I return in a couple of hours, only the tray is left, damp cells of dirt testifying to the fact plants were in them. Sara said the other day, watching the horde of hens rushing giddily at us, "Your chickens sure do love you, Gigi." I didn't have the heart to tell her that it has a lot more to do with food than love. Instead we made great dizzy loops around the yard with the silly ladies running at our heels until we tired of the game.

The first flight of geese went over low and fast this week, headed north. When I heard their high, wild call I barely had time to get outside before they vanished. Doubtless a flight of overachievers, anxious to be the first to return to the nesting grounds and get the very choice sites for brooding.

Tomato plants and peppers and a few herbs reside in the spare room waiting to be transplanted into the garden when the signs are right and the weather cooperates. Onions have been in for a long time, and the cilantro has begun to grow after its winter-over. I didn't know until this year that cilantro doesn't freeze out; at least it didn't this year. I've just been waiting for the mesquite tree to bud, thereby assuring me that there will be no more killing frost until next year. I believe she has, and so we will dig in the dirt and set the stage for The Perfect Tomato. Hope blooms eternal in the gardener's heart, renewable for no cost every spring.

And finally, the dreaded TAKS test is behind us, a happy harbinger of good times to follow. Both Grandson One and Grandson Two are in the third grade and had to take it this year. Grandson Two's mom called me, full of pride and relief, to say that he had done well and received a Commendable designation. Grandson One, much like his father, plays his cards close to the vest. When I asked him, after school, how he did, he looked surprised. You'd think by now he'd know I have my sources, but he said, with quirked eyebrows, "How did you know we had our scores?" I gave my standard answer, good since they were toddlers; "You'd be surprised what I know." He, too, had done well, also receiving a Commendable.

"What is commendable, anyway?" he asked. After I explained he said, "Oh. Kind of like a compliment."

You could say that. Too bad I can't think of any commendable things to say about the originators of the whole TAKS idea, but I have to go and plant tomatoes with my Superiorly Commendable grandchildren.

March promises spring and all it's beauty.

A Face Lit With A Million Watt Smile

Ranchers and farmers as a breed generally are gifted with trailer loads of optimism. How else to explain a person who invests several hundred hours of hard, dirty labor and several thousand dollars worth of seed and fertilizer in a big patch of dirt with the hope and expectation that it will grow a crop worth more than the investment?

It has to rain enough, but not too much, and at the right time. The temperature must be cool enough, but warm enough, for the plants to thrive and there must not be a large enough invasion of insects to be lethal to the growing plants. When all this maneuvering produces a crop, more hours of hard, dirty labor are invested in the hope that a fair price will be available for the finished product.

Farmers don't do this once in their lives, or even once in awhile. They do it every single year, sometimes on several fronts at once. They don't waver in their course or falter in their execution, though they do love to complain to one another, mostly about rain. There is perpetually not enough or, rarely, too much of the precious stuff.

The amazing thing is, no matter the outcome, their attitude is basically the same. If they have a good year, they hope next year is better. If the year's harvest is disappointing, they're certain next year will be better. The one thing they seldom ever do is chuck the whole frustrating process and get a job at Wal-Mart. All rain means there is that you get wet on the way in to work.

We're all lucky that farmers, and ranchers as well, seem to have an inexhaustible supply of optimism. Let's hope it recharges at least as well as the aquifers have so far.

It's something like that unquenchable optimism that fuels the quest for The Perfect Tomato most years. It didn't happen last year because the weather was so strange; tomatoes didn't do well in my garden at all. But I have received my first garden catalog, and since browsing the pages lush with astounding veggies requires far less effort than actually planting and tending them, my enthusiasm is at its customary January high.

As if to encourage my seed order, it is raining at last; too late for the oats, but good for everything else, including pasture and garden. Surely this year I will push aside bracts of pungent green leaves and find nestled there a tomato so perfect I will be moved to tears and unable to eat it, choosing instead to admire it enshrined on a plate. Rosy red and perfectly shaped, totally without scarring, catfacing, or any other tomato disaster, it will light up my kitchen with its glowing perfection.

Shall it be a hybrid from the grower, with all its attendant wilt and fungus resistance, or an heirloom, more susceptible to disease but superior in size, shape and flavor? Shall it be deep red, bright pink or even yellow? Nah, yellow's no good for the Perfect Tomato. It has to be red. Okay, we've narrowed it down to twenty pages of varieties, each sounding more luscious than the last.

I go through this every year and have yet to achieve my goal. I've been close, but no cigar – er – tomato. Still, I expect one day it will happen, that single fruit like no other before it, and to that end I keep planning and planting. We've had a lot of good eating, striving for that ultimate globe, and a lot of fun trying for it, thanks to optimism.

It doesn't seem that hard to maintain optimism on a farm. There are always new beginnings, new opportunities for growth and success, and half the fun is getting there. There are other situations in which we find ourselves that make optimism harder to come by, natural though those situations may be. One of those is aging. Everything living does it, but it's not a happy thing sometimes, and sometimes it can wring your heart so hard, you need a garden to go and sit in for a while until you can breathe again.

It often happens that children and animals show us the way to make it through a bad patch. On a recent visit to a nursing home to see dear folks newly admitted and very unhappy about it, Sara and

I encountered a little lady in a wheelchair in the hall. I had seen her before and though I smiled and spoke, she was unresponsive. This time, though, she called after us as we passed. "That sure is a wonderful little boy you have there."

We turned back to her. "Thank you," I said, "but this is my little granddaughter, Sara." Sara was studying the woman intently; she can be very shy with strangers and I didn't expect her to respond.

"I wish you'd come and see me sometime," the little lady said, and to my surprise Sara released my hand and ran the few feet to the lady's chair. Reaching up, she gave her the biggest hug she had, and the old woman's face lit with a million watt smile as she returned the embrace.

"You sweet, sweet baby," she said, and Sara ran back to me. "Come and see me again, will you?"

We promised to see her next time and went out into the cool, damp air, Sara chattering about jumping in rain puddles on the pavement, free to climb into the car and go about our business.

I was certainly optimistic about the rest of my day. I hope that Sara's smile and genuine, unaffected hug had made the little old lady's day easier, too.

Food For Conjecture On A Hot Afternoon

It's just way too hot to get physical in the middle of the day. Holding a water hose and watching the gurgling stream of clear well water disappear into a crack in the ground is about all I care to do. That leaves the mind floating free to ruminate on the myriad of wonders we encounter every day. Life is filled with small mysteries that, singly and apart, would hardly rock the world, but do offer a worthy opportunity for idle conjecture.

For instance: while I was doing laundry the other day, I had a brand new shirt to add to the load. I took it off the hanger and stood there unbuttoning the buttons all the way down the front and it occurred to me to wonder how all those buttons got buttoned up tight in the first place. Is there an assembly line of people who do nothing but button up shirts all day? If so, are their fingers really tough and callused, or do they wear finger stalls like post office guys did when they "pitched mail" into boxes in the back of the office for local delivery. Gloves, maybe? Or is there a machine that buttons x-number of shirts an hour, and what would that look like?

Ditto all those straight pins in new dress shirts. Do they have any purpose, real or imagined, other than frustrating the person attempting to open the shirt without drawing blood?

Why are young children programmed to regard anything they are in possession of for longer than five minutes as their exclusive property, never to be touched, looked at or spoken of by siblings? Said object then becomes the catalyst for a savage, all-out, take-no-prisoners war, even though there may be one or more exact duplicates of said object within easy reach. (The only answer ever received when questioning a child on this matter is: because it's mine!)

Why does a dog who never misses the opportunity to fling himself headlong into any body of water he encounters turn into a blithering idiot, throwing all 85 of his muscular pounds backward and digging furrows in the ground with all four huge feet, when he realizes I am about to put him in the tub for a bath? Is it something to do with clean water versus yucky goose water? (Guess which category he prefers.)

We all experience plenty of minor irritations every day; they blend into our daily routine. It sometimes seems as if some cosmic force with extremely bad timing or a warped sense of humor is at work. The phone rings just as you step into the shower. The baby wakes up the minute you lie down. Just as you sit down at the table with a cup of coffee and the paper, the dogs leap up from their

211

hours-long nap and make a dive for the cat, causing her to leap for the safety of your lap and miss. She snags the tablecloth instead and it all ends up in your lap, including the hot cup of coffee.

How does the calling party know you're dripping wet; what tips the baby that you're about to steal a nap? And why, when you have found a quiet moment, do dogs sleeping soundly 23 hours a day suddenly wake and rampage as a pack through the house after a cat they are accustomed to sleeping with? There are no ready answers.

Another exasperating dilemma: why do cats who live a comfortable, absolutely idyllic life in the house with ample food, plentiful water, toys and scratching posts and anytime access to the bed where their people sleep have a burning desire to go outside into the great world of cars and dogs and goodness-knows-what?

Example: Sebastian is a 15-pound rescue cat who has lived happily in the home of Grandson Two and Sara for over two years. He is a wonderful cat, much-loved and cared for. Besides being unbelievably handsome, with his butter-yellow fur, his green eyes and beatific smile, he has the heart of a true gentleman. Never once has he growled or scratched or even tried to escape the loving ministrations of the grandkids. But he is a paradox; deep within his soul burns the flame of the adventurer, and he sits at the door gazing with

212

undisguised longing at the dogs and cats coming and going outside. A couple of times he has escaped, but clearly is unsure in which direction to take his newly-found freedom and so is always quickly captured and returned to his gilded prison.

A few nights ago, however, he made good his escape and, on a particularly busy evening, was not missed. Early the next morning Grandson Two heard the dogs barking as if demented, their raucous voices counter pointed by the howls of a cat. Sebastian was in a bois d'arc tree, wedged into a crotch among wicked thorns with his forefeet stuck straight out before him. When ladders were brought and the grandsons retrieved him amid Sara's tears and much grownup coaching, it was discovered that several of his claws were gone, leaving bloodied holes behind. His pads were bloody, as well, and he would hobble only a few steps before flopping down with a pathetic expression on his face.

Dr. Saylor gave him a shot and some medicine to take until it's gone; Sebastian's reaction to it says it probably doesn't taste like tuna. The doctor said that he had seen cats' claws look like that when they had been bumped by a car and had gripped the road so hard it tore the claws out, and that Sebastian was probably a very lucky cat. What happened to him on his big night out? Sebastian isn't talking. Though he sits at the door and stares outside, he isn't trying to make a break for it any more.

More food for conjecture on a hot afternoon.

Sara and Sebastian

Traditions Slip Away

Many old traditions have gone by the wayside; barn raisings, corn husking bees, harvest dances. There aren't many people left who remember what big events those were in the everyday lives of folks, yet the old practice of cleaning up cemetery plots in the spring remains an important tradition in many small communities.

Years ago, the care of one's last resting place was in the hands of family and, incidentally, the subject of discussion in small towns where there wasn't a lot to talk about. If you didn't maintain your family plot in a decent manner, it was a blot on your name. If you couldn't do it, there was always a handyman available who would help out for a small fee. Most often, a couple of times a month the whole family went out to the cemetery on Sunday afternoons after church and dinner, armed with hoes and rakes, hoses and fresh flowers. Children played among the gravestones while adults weeded, planted and watered, talking quietly among themselves. It fostered a kind of connectedness, one generation to the next.

Perpetual care has relieved city dwellers of that chore, and many small town residents, too. Distance has always prevented participation for some family members, when the children have moved away. But in most small rural cemeteries, family members or members of a cemetery association take on the job.

It's nice to have traditions that anchor a bit of the past in the current sweeping us through the days now. Perhaps as one gets older that kind of thing is more important, but so much can be lost in the name of progress and "saving time" that is later seen to be more sacrifice than it seemed at the time.

A couple of days ago, on the way to Florence, we encountered men and big yellow machines in the process of pushing over a huge oak tree standing in the way of yet another stretch of road "improvement". Just down the road stood a pair of giant oaks with beautiful spreading branches, healthy leaf growth and perfect arching canopies. They have been there for many years and looked ready to stand many more. In an area where oaks are sick with wilt and decline, such trees are to be prized.

Not these. I actually felt sick at the thought of what was to come in a matter of minutes. The trees stood firm in the morning sun, the wind moving through them as it always had, right in the path of the big yellow machines. Across the road lies a mesquite pasture, but right next to that is a handsome pipe and wire fence on a very nice place. The trees lost.

Okay, I'm prejudiced. I am a confirmed tree hugger. But I'm also a "keep your mitts off our place" person, like lots of us in the country. There isn't a good solution, no way to balance "growth and progress" with keeping things the way they are. And I simply do not care if the county/state ever builds or "improves" another road for people to whiz from place to place on, because as soon as it gets built, people will find it and drive like maniacs on it. Sorry, that's not worth losing trees that took centuries to grow and taking chunks of land, in my humble opinion.

Just down from the tree slaughter, we crossed Berry's Creek on the big, nice bridge. I hate it. If you really try, you can see the stream flowing below. We used to go down into a low water crossing and drive through the water. You could stop and dip your hand in it or just watch it for a minute, waiting to see the silver minnows flash past your fingers. The kids from farms around close played in the swift, cool flow almost every hot summer afternoon while there was enough water running. Yes, there was a pool with a rope where they swung out and dropped in and that wasn't 50 years ago, either.

A little farther on we came to a long, level stretch of road where the bar ditches, normally bright, lush green at this time of year, are turning brown and ugly. They've been sprayed with poison so they won't have to be mowed. No grass, no flowers, no weeds, no mess. It's a bar ditch! Why does it have to be a barren gouge in the ground? If it's a traffic hazard, with grass and weeds so tall clear vision is obscured, that's one thing, but I don't see it.

My goodness, it's true. I must be getting old. I like quiet fields and green roadsides with wildflowers and big trees full of birds. I like free-flowing streams and low water crossings and natural underbrush full of small life you never see while zipping past at 50 mph. I hate seeing it all pushed over and ground up and leveled out and poisoned off.

I need a nap. That's another tradition on the edge of extinction for anyone over three and under 80, but I firmly believe more people should try it. Preferably on a warm afternoon looking up through the branches of a big, green tree.

If you can find one.

Epilogue

One never knows, when launching a new project, whether or not it will be a success. "Success", for me, is the realization that what I write is well-received and readers want to see more. This book is the first such project I have tried, and I have no real expectation to hit the *New York Times* best seller list with a million copies published. It would be lovely, but reality is far less ambitious. It is a dream of mine to establish a readership for the book such as has been accomplished with the column. I would appreciate your contacting me through my website www.eggsinmypocket.com and letting me know your evaluation of the book, the kind of subjects you find most interesting and whether you would have any interest in a sequel.

There are still plenty of pastures to be explored!

Printed in the United States
221445BV00002B/1/P